Acknowledgements

I have been fortunate to know and work with many people who have shaped my thinking over the past few years, people without whom this book would be much sparser and my life much less rich.

I owe a great debt to Neil Hopkin, the first head teacher I worked for, who has consistently helped me to see the balance between the ideal and the practical, helped me maintain and realise my ambitions, and encouraged me to question and seek out challenge.

I would also like to thank Nick Cooper, Simone Haughey, Zoe Case and others I worked with at Robin Hood School, without our conversations challenging the preconceptions of how we 'do school' much that is here would be lacking.

Many colleagues at Plymouth University have shaped my thinking through their work, our discussions and debates. Lorraine McCormack, Rachael Hinks Knight, Steve Wheeler, Orla Kelly, Roger Cutting, Pete Kelly and Nick Pratt have all introduced me to their perspectives and ideas that have shaped this book. I cannot thank Pete Yeomans enough, firstly for persuading me to make the move to Plymouth, secondly for his intellectual challenges, but mostly for being a dear friend who has helped me with figuring it out.

Many people have influenced me over the last five years through their blogs, tweets, and our all too occasional face to face discussions at events. Thanks to everyone who has shared their nuggets of insight, and their reflections on learning online.

Of those, I must particularly thank Ewan McIntosh, for his clear thinking on opening up learning to the challenges of the real world, Doug Belshaw for his ideas on Digital Literacy and ambiguity and Carl Gombrich whose ongoing thinking on the place of academic disciplines in the connected world has changed my thinking.

Many of the ideas in this book grew from posts on my blog, and most of those were prompted by the many young children I have worked with in schools and students at Plymouth University. I hope I have managed to develop your thinking as much as you have all developed mine, working with you has been a great privilege.

The final thanks must go to my family and friends for their support whilst writing this book, and always. Most of them have listened to me verbally working out ideas for this book many times, and have often helped me to see the wood for the trees. I am lucky that there are too many people here to name individually, but thanks to all of you for your support and friendship.

To my Mum and Dad I owe thanks for the obvious reasons, but also for bringing me up to value exploring possibilities, not getting stuck in boxes and thinking differently.

Praise for The Thinking Teacher

I was recently sat at the back of a secondary school classroom in a Middle-Eastern country waiting for the lesson to start. Why was I there? I was on a fact-finding mission to inform me of what might be needed for a curriculum development project I had been commissioned to undertake. I had asked to meet key stakeholders: education ministers, funders, teacher-education college lecturers, school teachers and students. The ministry was suspicious of me wanting to go into a school – they had asked me to write curriculum materials to a brief for teachers to 'deliver', but why would I want to consult with teachers, more so students? They relented as I had argued that it would help me create better materials if I understood the audience. So here I was. The teacher walked in to start the lesson, powered up the electronic whiteboard and started by going through his intended learning outcomes point by point. My heart sank – I could well have been in any classroom in England. The lesson was good in many respects, but formulaic and predictable. There isn't anything wrong with learning objectives, learning outcomes and success criteria per se, it is just that their mechanical use often leads to uninspiring teaching and passive learning. Let's have some more thought from teachers beyond the obvious. I was thus intrigued to receive *The Thinking Teacher* to review.

The Thinking Teacher is not a 'how to' book; indeed, Quinlan notes that 'there is no one model of a highly effective teacher, no one set of things that these people do to make things happen'. There are many good teachers who achieve good results by following a tried and tested repertoire of teaching approaches. Quinlan argues that what separates the truly great teachers from the good ones is that they truly understand learning and the different forms it can take; they spot opportunities for encouraging it in ways that they were never taught to do. These are the individuals who can adapt their teaching to the changing world that young people are in; these are the individuals that move teaching forward. These teachers think for themselves and get their pupils to think for themselves too. I could not agree more.

The book is divided into twelve chapters each exploring an aspect of schooling with intriguing titles such as 'All you need is love'; 'Technology as a mirror' and 'Learning as becoming', but each with a consistent argument: teachers should reflect on their own practice and students should think for themselves if their learning is to be deep and meaningful. In Chapter 2, Quinlan asks: 'What kind of teacher are you?' and explains that how you define yourself as a teacher is one of the most powerful areas to consider. Rehearsed are the typical tensions between progressives (characterised by Dewey as being more interested in expression, the cultivation of individuality and interacting with the world in a way that prepares young people for participation in a changing world) and traditionalists (who see education as the transmission of a body of knowledge and skills formulated in the past). Quinlan argues that asking questions that we already know the answers to simply reproduces the world as it is, or was, but by asking questions that we do not know the answers to can lead to change – either a change in how we interact with the world or about how we think about the way it works. Indeed, the argument of Chapter 6 is that replicating 'best practice' is not good enough as this is a retrospective exercise; rather we should strive for 'next practice', that is, the best practice of tomorrow.

There is a thoughtful section on reflection and references to Donald Schon's concepts of 'reflection on action' and 'reflection in action', which are now standard as part of the curriculum in many teacher-education institutions, and most teachers are encouraged to continue learning from their practice by reflecting on it afterwards and considering how they could move forward in terms of developing students. I also like the discussion of how much information we should supply learners to help them formulate problems and come up with solutions. There is a strong argument to give learners 'spaces to think'. On the use of silence, Quinlan writes: 'Imagine what would happen if when you asked a question you met the answer with silence. The result could be similar to providing thinking time before choosing a member of the class to answer.'

Following Mick Waters's excellent book *Thinking Allowed on Schooling* (2013), we now have another 'must buy' book for the thinking teacher: *The Thinking Teacher*. Continuing the same theme, Quinlan gets the reader to move on from thinking of 'learning as acquiring to learning as becoming'; in other words, he is advocating a classroom based around students becoming participants in the subject rather than possessors of certain, closely defined slices of it. This shift in thinking transforms a subject from a collection of knowledge or skills to be gained to a field of discussion, a community and a space.

Dr Jacek Brant, Institute of Education

This is not a teaching manual. It's not a guide to help you impress your senior leadership team or Ofsted. There are no checklists or worksheets. And you'd struggle to place it one side or the other of any of the either/or debates about education that are the current focus of so many pedagogues and politicians.

Quinlan doesn't have an axe to grind, nor a method to sell – he simply wants all of us involved in education to pause and take some time to think, properly, about what we're doing and, perhaps more importantly, why. Through a series of gently challenging essays, he questions ingrained assumptions, suggests avenues of mental exploration and encourages honest, open reflection. There are some practical ideas you could try out in your own classroom, but the main aim of this book is to inspire you to develop yourself as a 'thinking teacher', who will naturally help to nurture thinking children with the skills and aspirations to shape a truly successful and fulfilled future.

Helen Mulley, Editor, *Teach Secondary* magazine

'If we want thinking children, we need thinking teachers', says Oliver Quinlan at the start of his book. He's dead right – and systematically and skilfully he shows us what that means. The result is a book of considerable depth, yet written with a lightness of touch that makes it eminently readable. For me, now approaching my thirtieth year as a teacher, I learnt a huge amount that was new and was nudged to rethink ideas that I have for too long taken for granted as the only way of doing things. Like all the best education books, this one left me genuinely excited about my work as a teacher and thoroughly refreshed in my own thinking.

Geoff Barton, Head Teacher, King Edward VI School, Suffolk

Oliver Quinlan makes an impassioned plea in this manifesto for teachers and school leaders everywhere: don't stop thinking. He makes a convincing case that making time to think is not just the key ingredient of great learning, it's also in the make-up of our top teachers.

Ewan McIntosh, founder NoTosh.com

Oliver Quinlan

The Thinking Teacher

Independent Thinking Press

First published by

Independent Thinking Press
Crown Buildings, Bancyfelin, Carmarthen, Wales, SA33 5ND, UK
www.independentthinkingpress.com
Independent Thinking Press is an imprint of Crown House Publishing Ltd.

British Library Cataloguing-in-Publication Data

A catalogue entry for this book is available from the British Library.

Print ISBN 978-178135108-6
Mobi ISBN 978-178135151-2
ePub ISBN 978-178135152-9
ePDF ISBN 978-178135153-6

Printed and bound in the UK by

TJ International, Padstow, Cornwall

Contents

Acknowledgements . . . . *i*

Preface . . . . *v*

Introduction 1

1. All you need is love 19

2. Lenses for teaching 27

3. The futility of utility 37

4. Technology as a mirror 41

5. Quantifying learning 53

6. Best practice or next practice? 67

7. Regulation: lessons from finance 81

8. Minimum viable lessons 89

9. Worse is better 99

10. Learning as becoming 113

11. On inspiration 121

12. Don't settle 125

Conclusion 137

Further thinking 139

Bibliography 147

Preface

In one of those moments when you know you have been at something too long, I looked out of the library window. I was halfway through the reading list for my PGCE essay on managing children's behaviour and felt totally uninspired. I wondered, not for the first time, whether what was expected of me was to simply paraphrase all the instructions I was reading about how to control children. I thought teaching was going to be about more than this.

I moved on to the next book on the pile, opening the simple blue and orange cover expecting more instructions. This one was different; the author hadn't set out to tell me what to do, but to raise some questions and present some research on the evidence that might inform the answers. The case studies encouraged me to think about what effect the way the furniture in a classroom might affect how the children perceived it, raise questions about the messages that were being put across through the way tasks were designed, and question the assumptions I was making about how people think when implementing reward charts, even if they do appear to work ... This, I thought, is what teaching should be about; not ticking off the answers, but starting to think.

Several months later, as I walked off the stage, I felt a hand on my arm. Turning round, I saw a teacher whose blog I had been following for the past year and who had been giving me ideas for the classroom since I had started training to be a teacher. 'Great stuff,' he said, 'you really made me think differently about that; you took some research, thought about it and made it happen in your classroom. More of us should be thinking like that.'

I had found out about TeachMeets only a few months before, when I heard about a group of teachers who got together in Nottingham to share ideas that had worked in their classrooms. The empowering nature of them appealed to me and, as a newly qualified teacher in a school with a remit for trying new things, I was hungry for ideas I could develop. So, when I saw a similar get-together was happening at an education technology show I was going to, I signed up to attend, and without thinking too much about it, I also signed up to share an idea, just thinking that was the way it worked.

I did not expect to be picked by the random generator to be one of the first to present. I did not expect to stand on a stage in front of 300 people. I certainly did not expect for so many of those people to say I had made them think about taking perspectives from research to think differently about their teaching. That, I thought, is what teaching is about; not ticking off the next new idea, but always trying to think.

Some weeks later, I was teaching subtracting two-digit numbers, and I was demonstrating to the class of 8-year-olds how to use a hundred square to calculate the difference between 100 and any two-digit number. I was halfway through when Barnes put his hand up. So as not to confuse things, I thought I would come to his question once I had finished explaining. But Barnes couldn't wait, and he politely but assertively interrupted me. 'Mr Quinlan, please don't say "count down",' he said. 'It might be moving down the board but you are counting up in tens – that could really confuse some people.'

He knew what I meant, but he was thinking beyond that – thinking about the implications of the language I was using on the understanding of the rest of the class. That, I thought, is what teaching should be about; getting them thinking.

If we want thinking children, we need thinking teachers.

Introduction

This book is about thinking about teaching and learning. There is a lot of thinking that goes on in schools, in teachers' cars on the way to and from school, in their homes when planning, and in the holidays when reflecting on the term that has just gone and the one ahead. There is also a lot about teaching and learning that we do not think about so much, assumptions that are so ingrained we never question them, possibilities we never spot because we are so accustomed to the ways of schools.

There are few other careers than teaching where everyone entering already has thirteen years of experience in the workplace. There are tremendous strengths that come with this, but also tremendous problems because once you have spent so long immersed in something it is very difficult to see it in different ways. Education systems move very slowly, in part because we all have so much ingrained experience and memories that often we repeat the kind of teaching we experienced without thinking about it. Even if we aim to repeat only the best and forget the worst, it requires taking a step outside and some distance to see the different ways that teaching and learning might happen, ways which might just work better for our changing young people and changing society than those that suited us in a time that is already ancient history to them.

Here, I want to share some possible avenues to those different ways, some challenges to the assumptions we make and some perspectives from outside to encourage new thinking. This book is not about telling you how things should be done, what new forms of teaching should look like or where education should be going. This book is an invitation to start to build the answers to those questions, to think them through and see where they might go. It is an invitation to seek out challenges and perspectives that, in the hectic life of teaching, you might not see unless you take the time out to see them, and to keep looking for more.

There are many incredible teachers out there, teachers who get others excited about their subject, who open up opportunities to young people by developing their knowledge and skills, and who make their students aspire to great things. Amongst these individuals there are a huge range of outlooks, ways of teaching and ways of thinking about what they do. There is no one model of a highly effective teacher, no one set of things that these people do to make things happen. Thinking back to the teachers that made a big impression on me, there were those that created exciting and unusual lessons, but also those that were very traditional. There were those that were very approachable and friendly, but also those that we never chatted to informally but that had high expectations and made us live up to them. As teachers, this is both exciting and frustrating: frustrating in that there is no clear, step-by-step model that we can follow, but exciting in that it is something that we can make our own, something that is more about who you are than any instructions that you follow.

What is more important than the specific things that teachers do is the ways in which they think. There are some good teachers who have a bank of different things they do that they know work, and deploy these over and over without thinking too much about them. It is more than possible to get good results by doing this, particularly if the context of your teaching does not change too much. What marks the truly great teachers from the good ones is that they are not leafing through a library of strategies, they just get it. They really understand learning and the different forms it can take; they spot opportunities for encouraging it in ways that they were never taught to do. These are the individuals who can adapt their teaching to the changing world that young people are in; these are the individuals that move teaching forward. It is not just about a limited palette of what they know – it is about how they think.

The kind of person you are, the way you think; these are not the kinds of things we usually consider changing or working on. They are the kinds of attributes possessed by people who come to things naturally, people who just think differently, people who just 'get it'.

If we are in the business of teaching and learning we have to believe that most things are learnable. All things being equal, it is possible to make significant changes in yourself and to learn. Of course, many things are situational: I am never going to be an Olympic gymnast – I am too old and my body is past it already. However, with enough time, dedication and practice I could certainly learn some gymnastic skills and improve.

Thinking is no different. We tend to give great credence to the idea that our thinking and intelligence is quite fixed, but many researchers are now exploring what optimistic teachers have thought forever: intelligence is much more complex than being born smart.[1] Given some attention and some belief in the power of learning it can be developed in many ways.

This book is about thinking differently about teaching, about taking the time to question our assumptions and the things we don't always take the time to consider. It is about opening our eyes to the changes and contrasts in the world that might influence the way we think about learning, and not accepting things as they are but looking to what they could be.

---

1 G. Claxton and B. Lucas, *New Kinds of Smart: How the Science of Learnable Intelligence is Changing Education* (Maidenhead: Open University Press, 2011).

Who do we remember?

I work with student teachers and when interviewing prospective new students I often get a fascinating insight into the motivations people have for becoming a teacher. It is always interesting hearing their answers to the question, 'Why do you want to become a teacher?', largely because they are all so similar. Of course, an interview situation is far from scientific – prospective students are hardly going to tell me it is for the holidays. Even if the situation did allow them to be more candid, the vast majority of people do seem to go into the profession because they care, because they really want to make a difference.

Often people cite positive reasons for going into teaching and occasionally they are spurred on by negative experiences at school – wanting to provide children with the education 'they didn't have'. What is common to both of these very different approaches is the desire to be a teacher that students remember. Most people have very strong memories of certain teachers, and it strikes me that in most cases this correlates with the 'difference' that individuals starting out as teachers set out to make.

It could be argued that any moderately successful teaching constitutes 'making a difference'. A child comes to you unable to read; the lessons you teach them and the experiences you provide them with means that at the end of their time with you they can read. A difference has been made. Reading is a profound example, given how central it is to schooling and life in general, but the same is true for less fundamental things. Understanding a scientific concept such as condensation, knowing the reasons why an election in a democracy works in the way it does, being able to select the colours needed to create a desired artistic effect; making any kind of learning happen is creating a difference. Making such differences is not necessarily difficult – although causing these differences to happen consistently and regularly for all learners in the large classes most people teach takes skill – but all teachers make some kind of difference. In his comprehensive review of educational research, John Hattie found that everything and anything a teacher does has an impact.[2]

However, it is not these small differences that the prospective teachers I interview are talking about. Causing a small change in someone's memories does not a memorable teacher make. Think about the teacher or teachers you remember and why they stand out. Generally, the teachers people remember are ones that they perceive to have made a bigger difference – a difference that has affected the way they think.

Sometimes this is for academic reasons, but it is usually about an individual who really engaged them through their teaching. This could be by simply being enthusiastic about their subject, but sheer enthusiasm alone is unlikely to engage students in such a way they continue with that subject. For teachers to be memorable, they also have to present the subject in such a way that their students can understand it, see its relevance, enjoy its challenge and get enthusiastic about it themselves. These memorable teachers open up their subject to others, often in a way that causes them to pursue the subject, or a related field, further and always in a way that allows them to use that subject as a different lens to look at the world.

Sometimes the reasons are more personal. Many people remember teachers who helped them to develop in a personal sense. This can be through supporting them through a particularly difficult time or by their approach to life – the way they engender confidence in their students, the way they encourage them to see the problems and challenges they face differently.

Whether your idea of what a memorable teacher should be is based on the academic, the personal, or something in between, memorable teachers are those who make us think differently.

2 J. Hattie, *Visible Learning: A Synthesis of Over 800 Meta-Analyses Relating to Achievement* (London: Routledge, 2008).

The teachers we remember are the ones who cause a shift in our thinking about something we value, who in some way change the way we think about ourselves or the world.

What is thinking?

Entire books can and have been written on the subject of thinking. The question is potentially a philosophical one – considering what makes a thought a thought – or a scientific or neurological one – considering what physically happens in people's brains when they think. For the purposes of this book, I am working on cognitive psychologist Daniel T. Willingham's broad but concise definition that thinking is: 'solving problems, reasoning, reading something complex, or doing any mental work that requires some effort'.[3] My focus is particularly on the idea of thinking in terms of solving problems, and thereby generating solutions to those problems.

Thinking is often presented as something that we are doing all of the time, but it is worth considering the difference Willingham draws between *thinking* and *remembering*. He states that whilst we might consider ourselves to be thinking all of the time, thinking is actually something we naturally do as little of as possible. In comparison to memory, thinking is slow and unreliable so we will always try to rely on memory which is much faster and less likely to be wrong.

Consider solving a simple maths problem, such as how many items you have in ten groups of five. To work this out from scratch requires some thought. If you already know how to count in fives then it might not take too long, but if you really want to start from scratch you would

3 D. T. Willingham, Why Don't Students *Like* School? Because the Mind Is Not Designed for Thinking, *American Educator* (Spring), 4–13. Available at: www.aft.org/pdfs/americaneducator/spring2009/WILLINGHAM%282%29.pdf, p. 4.

probably need to draw your ten groups, draw five objects in each and then count them up. This is considerably slower and more prone to error than knowing the sequence of counting in fives and moving through it ten places, or just knowing your five times table. You could perhaps use some other knowledge to shortcut this even further by using the maths teacher's least favourite trick of simply adding a zero to a number when multiplying it by ten. What is more likely when I presented this problem to you is that you bypassed all of these by simply knowing that five multiplied by ten is fifty.

At one time it was conceivably possible for a very clever individual to think through from first principles all of human knowledge, but this has not been the case for a very long time. There is no way we can consider the fundamentals of everything humans know, so as well as relying on our own memory; we also rely on that of other people. We learn the solutions to problems that they have found by reading what they have written or by having someone else tell us about their discoveries. We can have the thought processes behind these facts demonstrated to us to help us understand how they got there, but once we are there we also rely on memory to recall this information rather than thinking it through again. This is hugely important to the development of our knowledge and understanding; without having the work of others to build on in this way, our understanding would never have developed to where it is.

Newton famously said of his scientific discoveries, 'If I have seen further it is by standing on the shoulders of Giants', acknowledging that his new thinking was entirely built on the work of those who had thought things through before him. We are all standing on the shoulders of giants each and every day. There are vast swathes of our everyday lives that we have never thought about; we have been told or shown how they work by others, who have been told or shown how they work in their turn, and so on, from someone who solved the problem by thinking it through, often a long time ago. This passing on of knowledge is one of the reasons why humans are so successful and it is fundamental to how we live; using the knowledge of others who solved problems is much more reliable than working things out for ourselves.

The problem is that memory is so good that it stops us from thinking, so knowledge gets passed on and passed on, sometimes without anyone considering if there might be another, better way. When people do notice that the ways we do things are perhaps not as good as they might be and consider them again, we get change. In some circumstances, the unreliability and unpredictability of thinking something through can be a strength because it produces different solutions. Sometimes these alternative solutions are worse than the ones we had been using, but occasionally this process results in better solutions.

This book takes the premise that it is usually useful to think again, to challenge the assumptions that we build up by relying on transmitted memories. On occasion, this leads us to realise that the answer we already had was a very good one, so it was worth it just to confirm this and to better appreciate why this is so. At other times, we may come to appreciate that there are better ways to do things, so we move forward and produce new perspectives that change the way we think about things and what we do.

We get there by asking questions, by looking at contrasts and asking why things work in some situations and not in others, and by asking that most challenging question of all, 'why?'

Questioning and subversion

The reasonable man adapts himself to the world: the unreasonable one persists in trying to adapt the world to himself. Therefore all progress depends on the unreasonable man.

George Bernard Shaw

Most teachers ask hundreds of questions every day – as a profession we know the value of questions. Questions let us know how our lesson is being received, whether we need to adjust the pace or expand our explanations. Questions prompt learners to have a go at things themselves, find out more or demonstrate their learning. Questions are also used for perhaps less valuable aims, showing us who is paying attention and getting students to think about what they have done wrong.

We ask a lot of questions of other people, sometimes closed, sometimes more open. Plenty has been written about the benefits of asking open questions to make students think, but usually even these are questions to which we already know the answer. We might begin a topic or a lesson by asking open questions; we know the answers to them, but we want to work out what the children know already so we can build on it. We might ask such questions throughout a lesson based on things we have just explored. We often ask them at the end of some learning to recap, draw attention back to key points and check they have gone in.

How often do you ask questions designed to actually make students think? Often our teaching is based on the subject content we are working with or the skills we are trying to develop. We split this up into key points or stages and structure the lesson to move through these. To construct lessons, and therefore also questions, around not the shape of the content but the shape of the thinking we want students to take is a subtle difference, but one which can have a profound effect.

These kinds of questions are the basis of the ancient method of teaching proposed and practised by Socrates, who famously used questions to prompt thinking. The basis of Socratic questioning is asking questions that refine thinking.

Firstly, imagine your initial understanding or ideas around a topic. We all usually bring something to the table when learning something new, but these ideas tend to be quite loose and broad before we understand much about it. Next, visualise your ideas across a wide area – the refined understanding is in there somewhere, but it is not yet well defined.

A Socratic questioner will choose one edge of the area and ask a question that challenges it – a question that can be as simple as 'Do you really think this?' Considering this question makes you realise, on reflection, that part of the concept is not what you really think, so the idea shrinks a little to reflect this and become more precise. The questioner then asks a question about a situation that fits with another edge of the concept and it shrinks again. The questioner repeats this with another challenge, and if the challenges are well judged and the answers well considered, then the idea continues to shrink until it reaches a much more refined and specific shape, constituting a more refined and specific understanding with the ambiguities removed.

These kinds of questions can be very powerful, and can even be asked by someone who doesn't know the end answer, but who can develop their own understanding from the increasingly refined answers given to their questions. They just have to be good at spotting the edges and asking challenging questions. I use the word 'just' cautiously, for this can be more difficult than actually having an understanding of the topic in question, and in some situations it can take courage to ask such challenging questions.

However, the fact that this is 'just' based on challenge and edge-spotting means that it is possible to ask Socratic questions even of yourself, and

in areas in which you do not yet know the answers. Take a subject that you think you understand and then consider what are the edges, the areas for which it would not work and why this is. Refine the idea so that it no longer includes these areas, or so that it works with them. Repeat. I find it helps to imagine someone who awkwardly disagrees with you on a regular basis (unless you are lucky enough to know such a person!).

If you are happy with your teaching as it is then there is perhaps no need to worry about Socratic questions; it all depends on whether you think being happy with things as they are is what education is about.

Many have theorised about the purpose of education. In one of the seminal works on this topic, French sociologists Pierre Bourdieu and Jean-Claude Passeron depicted our current education systems as being entirely about reproducing what already exists.[4] They asserted that education is all cultural reproduction and is structured in this way to ensure that the 'dominant culture' of our society is replicated and instilled in young people. This, they argued, is why certain groups do better in school than others; those whose backgrounds are closest to the dominant culture already have the cultural and social capital necessary to succeed.

As academics, Bourdieu and Passeron aimed to describe, without necessarily judging, how things are rather than whether or not they are right. Plenty of people before and since have been vociferous in their critique of this analysis, in which some groups are advantaged and some disadvantaged for educational success. Of course, there have been many initiatives to try to encourage social mobility by making education more accessible to those who do not have the cultural or social capital of their more advantaged peers.

However, some have argued that our notion of educational success is not very useful, and that schools should be about something more than

4 P. Bourdieu and J.-C. Passeron, *Reproduction in Education, Culture and Society*, tr. Richard Nice (London: Sage, 1990 [1970]).

simply reproducing the dominant culture. This argument recently reappeared in the shape of calls to recognise the changing nature of our world due to communications and technology, and a need to prepare young people for a future where there are no such things as 'right' answers. The pace of technological change may have hastened and spread this argument, but it has been around in some form for many years. In 1970, Neil Postman and Charles Wiengartner argued that the purpose of education should be the reverse of cultural reproduction; they said it should be a process of questioning the dominant culture in order to shape it into something fit for purpose.[5] In *Teaching as a Subversive Activity*, they suggest that education is one of the few institutions that is more invested in the future than the past, and teachers and students should be questioning the way things are and thereby shaping them anew for the future.

Postman and Wiengartner contend that subversion is a word steeped in negative connotations because it involves questioning the status quo and revealing what things could be; it therefore threatens those with vested interests in how things are, which is inevitably those with the most wealth and influence in our society. Rather than preparing people to live in society as it is, they argue that, through questioning, education should encourage young people to interrogate the existing status quo, to generate new thinking and to move society forward.

Similar arguments have been put forward more recently by Keri Facer, who explores the changing nature of relationships between the generations to make a case for education as a place for imagining the future rather than merely preparing young people for it.[6] In our world of increasing change, she maintains that many of the skills now required for success in adult workplaces are those that have traditionally been seen as the attributes of childhood. Flexibility, creativity, the ability to question, to see problems in new ways, to play with ideas before

---

5 N. Postman and C. Weingartner, *Teaching as a Subversive Activity* (London: Penguin, 1970).

6 K. Facer, *Learning Futures: Education, Technology and Social Change* (London: Routledge, 2011).

dismissing them and to learn and relearn; all of these attributes of success are things that many young people already do well. This fact, and their adeptness with the new technologies that are reshaping our world, Facer argues, gives young people an agency that they have not had for some time. This means that schools are ideal institutions in which to begin building the future rather than merely preparing for it.

It is by asking questions, and by being willing to be subversive, that people shape their world. In some cases, questioning the validity of something that is assumed to be 'just the way things are' can reveal that things could, in fact, be quite different. In other cases, this questioning reveals the deep and very sensible reasons why 'the way things are' should remain. In either case, the questioner is left with an informed perspective on the subject; even if it does not lead to change in the situation in question, it does lead to a development of their understanding.

Asking questions that we already know the answers to simply reproduces the world as it is, or was. Asking questions that we do not know the answers to can lead to change – either a change in how we interact with the world or about how we think about the way it works.

How often in your classes do you ask questions that you don't know the answer to? In some subjects, exploring the current edge of the field comes more easily than others. Geography, politics and science are all undergoing huge changes that hit the news on a daily basis, but all subject areas are changing at a rapid pace and there are new, relevant questions to be asked. Clearly, dealing with questions at the cutting edge requires background knowledge and understanding; the key is learning these as part of an engagement with the state of things now, and how they could be.

It is all about finding those questions at the edge – the challenges that matter – and learning what already exists to deal with them. Great teachers are immersed in their field, not as a syllabus but as a changing,

developing entity, with new areas to discover and new questions to ask. This is why, in any subject, the background is important but it is only a tool to enable the really interesting part – asking new questions and finding new answers.

How often do you, as a teacher, ask yourself questions that you do not know the answer to? Whether within your subject, or about how you teach, new perspectives develop from challenge, from taking the things that do not seem to fit in your box of ideas and using them to cultivate new ideas. Sometimes your own Socratic questioning is enough, and sometimes experiences in the classroom that did not work as expected can provide considerable challenge to refine your ideas, if you take the time to consider the implications.

Often, however, challenge has to be sought out and that is the central aim of this book. I have found that seeking out contrasts can create the challenge needed to refine thinking about teaching and learning. Sometimes you agree with ideas, sometimes you disagree; the important thing is that they make you think and move your ideas forward into something clearer.

For the thinking teacher such challenges should be welcomed. It is only by asking the questions that new knowledge raises that we are able to refine our thinking, and therefore what we do. If we are doing our job well, then our students will experience novel challenges and unknown questions every day. If we are to be model learners – those with the experience, empathy and knowledge to guide them through these challenges – then we need to make a deliberate effort to think regularly in questioning ways ourselves.

Thinking makes it so

... there is nothing either good or bad, but thinking makes it so.

Shakespeare, *Hamlet*

A problem will challenge with questions and, as with subversion, these words often have negative connotations. This is particularly the case when questions are applied to established institutions, such as schools, which have an inherent authority and respect, and which it can be seen as wrong to question.

The value of all things comes from interpretation, so what you value will therefore depend on your point of view and the context. Hamlet is referring to the moral dimensions of our actions – it is down to the individual or group to decide whether a certain action is morally just or unjust, good or bad. The same can be true of ideas and concepts; there are no inherently good or bad ideas, simply those that are useful or those that are not, and this generally depends on the way you think about them.

'Good' ideas – that is to say, those that you agree with or appear to be descriptive of how your world works – clearly have value. They can illuminate your understanding of how something works, and then take that understanding to the next level. Good ideas often give us the feeling that they are common sense, that they speak to the way we perceive and understand the world. After having accepted a good idea, it is often very difficult to remember how we perceived things before we encountered them. Good ideas are usually the easiest to take on and understand. Sometimes they may jar with previous things we thought we knew, sometimes making them seem wrong or no longer of value. It can be hard to throw old ideas away or rethink them, but sometimes an excellent idea comes along that seems to be so true, so good, that we are willing to do this. Indeed, if the idea is that good, it is almost impossible not to let go of some of what we previously believed about the way things are.

However, there is also a value in 'bad' ideas, the kind of ideas that we disagree with, that do not fit with our experience and knowledge, and grate in a way that seems unhelpful. These ideas are useful, even if only because thinking about how and why we feel this way can temper and strengthen the ideas that we do hold to be true and allow to influence us. The ideas we ultimately choose to disagree with and discard provide a counterpoint to the ideas that are 'good' and easier to accept.

The illusionist and entertainer Derren Brown puts this well in his book *Tricks of the Mind*.[7] In explaining his background and his work, he systematically debunks practices such as hypnotism, neuro-linguistic programming and even religion, yet he goes on to describe why all these practices are useful, indeed pivotal, to his ability to create the illusion of 'controlling' people. What matters is not whether he thinks these ideas are correct or not, but what light their existence sheds on how people conceptualise human behaviour and how he can take advantage of this.

Consider the idea of learning styles – that there are three types of learning: visual, auditory and kinaesthetic (VAK) – and that people have a preference for one of these styles. This theory has been discredited by all manner of people, from teachers who have found it does not fit with their own experiences, to learning theorists and neuroscientists.[8] Despite being a 'bad' idea, which has a questionable scientific basis, the theory has been highly influential and resulted in a range of different practices in schools. This is in no small part down to the fact that, on the surface, it appears to fit with common sense and is therefore an easy idea to swallow. Everyone has experiences of learning in these different ways and many people have certain preferences; they like it when teachers use visuals to explain things or when they are set up to learn by doing. Learning styles have therefore become quite widely accepted. The problem is that there is no clear link between what you like and how

---

7 D. Brown, *Tricks of the Mind* (London: Transworld, 2006).

8 P. Howard Jones, *Introducing Neuroeducational Research: Neuroscience, Education and the Brain from Contexts to Practice* (London: Routledge, 2009).

successfully you learn. Learning styles theory confuses personal prefer-ence with impact.

Even though the idea might be fundamentally a bad one, different results have transpired from teachers taking learning styles on board and attempting to use them in the classroom. On one hand, teachers have subjected the young people they work with to tests to find their preferred 'style', thereby labelling them as a particular type of learner and potentially limiting the effectiveness of their learning. Those labelled auditory learners might succeed when trying to learn some concepts that are best suited to this medium, but struggle with others. Try learn-ing to play golf, or any other physical skill, by having someone talk you through it on the telephone and without actually using the clubs.

On the other hand, the assimilation of learning styles by some teachers has resulted in them thinking about how certain learning is presented visually, aurally or through firsthand experience, and where practicable to set up their lessons to include a variety of these approaches, thus resulting in a range of media and activities in their classroom. At the very least, this approach maintains interest and attention; at best, it can result in ideas being communicated in forms which are most appropriate to their content, therefore accelerating the development of understand-ing by learners. Despite both approaches being based on a 'bad' idea, one clearly contains detrimental elements whilst the other has more positive outcomes.

What is important, therefore, is not leaving such things to chance. Novel theories can prompt practice in the classroom that is both good and bad, so considering any ideas we come across deeply is the only way to make certain that what happens in your classroom is constructive. It is either that or leave our impact on learners to luck.

There are no inherently good ideas or bad ideas, but thinking makes them so. What you do with them, and how thinking about them

influences your actions, is what is important. Sometimes the ideas that seemed bad at first are merely challenging but otherwise good. Sometimes those that seemed good on the surface are actually bad. This book contains many ideas; some may seem good to you and others bad. The important thing for the thinking teacher is that all ideas encourage us to think, and as a result can influence what is really important – what we do with them.

And so, good or bad, now to the questions, the contrasts and the thinking.

Chapter 1

All you need is love

Why are you a teacher? This question clearly has a vast landscape of answers, but many of them involve the concept of or the word 'love'. Teaching can be hard work, but the majority of teachers gladly take this on because they 'love the job'. For some this means loving the enthusiasm and energy of working with children and young people, for others it is about performance, for others again it is the sense of achievement they obtain from seeing someone 'get it'. The 'light bulb moment' is powerful, equally so for the person whose teaching allows the light bulb to go on as well as for those who see more clearly as a result.

Being in a job you love is a great privilege. It also seems, on the face of it, like a fairly pure intention; if you do something because you love it then that implies you are not doing it for the money. With the driving force of money, many people would argue, comes the potential for selfishness and corruption (although it must be remembered that whilst teaching may be perceived to be behind other professions, such as medicine, in the remuneration stakes, school teachers in the UK do not exactly work for free). Loving your job is a joy. It can give you tremendous energy for the long hours and the setbacks, not to mention adding much enjoyment to your days.

The problem with building a career solely on what you love is that falling in love is easy and seductive, but staying in love is quite another matter. A Department for Education paper in 2010 reported that five years after training almost fifty per cent of teachers in England were no longer teaching in state-maintained schools.[1] Staying in love with this job is hard.

As someone who went into teaching quite young, I felt that loving working with children was a big driver for my choice of career, as it seemed to be for many of my fellow students when I was training. It can be a joy to work with children – their energy and enthusiasm are contagious and they often see the world in different, interesting and thought-provoking ways. Conversely, that energy and enthusiasm can cause a whole lot of tension for those who don't appreciate it. This can be seen in the adverse reactions of those who clearly don't love working with children if they are ever put into a classroom situation or even just survive a children's birthday party. When working with children, it helps if you are able to cope with a bit of chaos sometimes; it helps a lot if you are able to actually appreciate it. Children are full of delight, so in the early days it is easy to fall in love with a job that involves sharing in their enthusiasm for the world.

We have a word for people who do something just for the love of it – amateurs. This word is also used to describe someone who is inexperienced or incapable, although this is not necessarily the case. Being an amateur does not preclude someone from being very good at what they do. In fact, the hours of experience, driven only by personal passion, can result in very skilled individuals. To see such people we only need look at the worlds of the arts and sport. Individuals who have developed a skill purely for the love of it might seem like an attractive proposition, but ask yourself whether, if you had something important that needed to be done, you would rather a professional or an amateur undertook it. Of course, it depends what that task is and whether there is a genuine choice, but for something as important and as long term as educating your children, most people would choose the professional. Whilst

---

1 Department for Education, *A Profile of Teachers in England from the 2010 School Workforce Census*. Ref: DFE-RR151 (2010). Available at: dera.ioe.ac.uk/11897/1/DFE-RR151.pdf.

amateurs may have the skills and the passion, we are living in a world increasingly characterised by the specialisation of roles, so without taking on something full time it is very difficult to build up the necessary experience and expertise in an area. Amateurs are not our first choice because they are part-time practitioners – they need to do other things to earn their living. As such, it is often perceived that they will probably not have the required commitment or incentive to stick at it when things get tough. This is probably unfair to many of the skilled amateurs out there, but that is the general perception – that having a love for something is not enough to guarantee seeing it through to completion.

So, if love is not a firm enough basis for building a career, then what is? My thinking on this has been influenced by ex-Apple interface and software designer Bret Victor. In his talk 'Inventing on Principle', he begins by renouncing the idea that people should define their career by 'following their passion' or 'doing something they love'.[2] Victor clearly loves creating digital tools – his enthusiasm for creatively manipulating computer code shows through despite his unassuming manner – but that is not enough to drive what he does. Being driven by a love of creating tools would only propel him to create for the sake of it, and not necessarily to develop the innovative and influential designs that have defined his career.

Rather than love, Victor argues that our careers should be driven by following a principle – 'something that you believe is important, necessary and right, and using it to guide what you do'. Whilst we may be able to fall in love, it is much harder to stumble across a principle; to develop one takes time, experience and thinking.

The strength of basing what you do around a guiding principle is that, by being well thought through, it is much harder to shake than something based purely on love. The daily grind can cause you to fall out of love

---

2 B. Victor, Inventing on Principle [video] (2012). Available at: www.youtube.com/watch?v=PUv66718DII.

with something, and it is hard to retain that light-hearted enthusiasm associated with love when faced with targets, inspections and challenge. A principle, however, is based on something deeper, something tangible that you are trying to achieve, something which despite challenges can remain an aim to strive for.

Part of the reason that a principle is hard to come by is that it needs to be specific enough to have meaning, yet general enough to be applied to everything you do. A general principle for a teacher could simply be for the young people they work with to learn. Whilst this is in many ways a laudable aim, I would argue that it is too general to be of use each day in the classroom. Think for a moment of the many 'vision statements' with which schools choose to subtitle their prospectuses and websites. Most of them could not be argued with; 'preparing students for the future', 'developing the whole child' and similar statements are full of promise, but you have to question how often they genuinely shape what happens in each classroom, each interaction that a teacher has with a young person.

As a designer of computer interfaces, Bret Victor's principle could be to simply make something new or to push things forward. On the face of it, these would be good aims for making a difference in his field or as a way to get his name noticed. However, his principle is much more specific: 'creators need an immediate connection to what they are creating'. This principle isn't focused on the applications that he develops, but the experience of the people who will use them and how the process works; something that he can bear in mind at every stage in the process. By being more specific, he has found a principle that shapes *all* of his actions, and as a result he has built a career that has led to genuine innovation.

Education *is* a field built from principles. Almost everyone involved in education has a commitment to the principle of educating children. The problem is that there are so many different interpretations of what the concept of education actually means that it needs to be defined more precisely. Walking into a classroom each day and aiming to educate is not going to provide a real focus unless the goal is more specific. To some teachers, education is about building a deep appreciation for their subject and how it matters in the world; to others it is about preparing young people for specific future careers; whilst others would define it as opening students' eyes to the way the world works and the opportunities it presents. How would you define it?

One educational organisation that is based around a strongly defined principle is the charity Teach First, which recruits high-achieving graduates to work in 'challenging' schools. Their principle is that 'no child's educational success is limited by their socio-economic background',[3] which is backed by a set of five values that are set out in detail and to which everyone in the organisation must sign up. What is interesting about their ethos is that despite recently becoming the single biggest recruiter of new graduates in the UK,[4] it immediately limits the scope of their work. Teach First is clearly focused on the achievement of children traditionally limited by their socio-economic background, which focuses them on particular demographics, areas (and therefore only some schools) and the target of 'educational success'. Not jobs, not earnings, not ambiguous notions of 'preparedness for the future', but educational success. This is further defined in their mission statement as meaning achievement in maths and literacy at primary school, GCSEs at secondary, and university graduation. Whether or not you agree that these are worthy goals, Teach First and their teachers have a precise set of principles they can aspire to, focus on and take into the classroom every day. The organisation also expends considerable effort trying to ensure that everyone they take on agrees that these are worthy goals – they aim to recruit people who are working towards the same, closely defined end.

---

3 See www.teachfirst.org.uk/AboutUs/.

4 See Science Guide, Teach First Top Recruiter (15 July 2013). Available at: www. scienceguide.nl/201307/teach-first-top-recruiter.aspx.

When you are ground down by the intensity of the job and the hours are taking their toll, holding on to the fact that you love your job can sometimes help. However, if you are experiencing more than a brief period of stress then this becomes a matter of cognitive conflict. It is the job that is making you feel this way, so holding on to the fact that you love it is hard – clearly, at the moment, you do not or it would not be causing you stress. A principle is not about whether you love something or not, but what you are trying to achieve by doing it. A principle is not fundamentally challenged by how hard it is; in fact, if a job is worthwhile it *should* be hard – the challenge of the situation often only makes it stronger.

Working with children and young people can be an exciting experience that fills you with energy, but sometimes it can sap that energy like nothing else. If loving working with young people is the underpinning purpose of what you are doing, this will be pretty hard to sustain at those times when that very thing is the source of your frustrations. If, on the other hand, you are underpinned by the principle of preparing young people to succeed in society, then often the very things that are frustrating you about their behaviour are the issues that need to be addressed to achieve your purpose. It might be a challenge, but without it there would not be the opportunity to address how they might learn to work with each other, or with you, without creating such stress.

A principle is also something to hold on to when the job is going in a direction that was perhaps not what you intended when you signed up to it. When the paperwork, inspection pressures or politics mount up, it is easy for the career you love to become hard to like. If that is why you are there, then it can be hard to stay, but a deeper principle can give you the sense of satisfaction to get through the difficult times.

Strong though it might be, a principle is not an all-sustaining panacea. It is not going to keep you in a situation that is no longer right for you. In fact, basing your career on a principle might make it more obvious when you are in an organisation or a situation that is inappropriate for you. If your principle is not aligned with the people you work with or the organisation you work for, then it could be time to seek out somewhere new. Equally, approaching the choice of new jobs with this in mind can be a useful tool for finding the right place to work. It is often very difficult, as a teacher, to get a feel for what working in a particular school will be like. More often than not, the decision will be based on what will always be a rather artificial tour of the school by one of its leadership team, and the equally artificial experience of teaching a lesson on an interview day. Unless you have managed to do some temporary work there first, the choice of whether to take up a job offer can be a shot in the dark. The clearer you are on your principles, the more prepared you will be to make judgements on this. Everything you see in your brief visit can be compared with what you will have already defined as important, and the clearer you are, the more straightforward it will be to decide whether what you see fits with what you believe.

Career paths can be messy, and not everyone gets the chance to rigorously define their principles and goals like organisations such as Teach First. Individuals come into teaching for all sorts of reasons, at all sorts of times in their lives and are not always given the opportunity or the encouragement to explore their convictions. Regardless of when in a career it happens, defining your principles is something everyone should do, because to be really effective at anything requires a focus. So, if you have a strong principle for what you are doing, write it down now; if you don't yet, then start thinking. We all have a vague feeling about what we are aiming for, but it needs to be articulated to make it specific enough to work with. Once you have written it down, take a look at it from the point of view of someone else and ask yourself if they could challenge you on what an element of it actually means. Keep on refining it until it is clear, and remember that this might mean making it more limited in scope. Do not fall into the trap of many school mission statements of trying to say everything and therefore saying nothing. What you come up with will probably have been there all along, but moving it from a feeling to a statement helps to distil it and transform it into something that you can apply every day.

Of course, your principles will shift and change over time; as new challenges are faced and further questions are asked they will develop and sometimes end up radically altered. What matters is that they *are* considered and defined, that the principles which underpin what you do can be returned to and drawn on in the difficult times. The result of this process will be a direction and a purpose that can meet those challenges and questions. Loving what you do is the fun part, but teaching should rest on firm principles that keep you doing what you love even when love is not enough.

Chapter 2
Lenses for teaching

What kind of teacher are you? How you define yourself as a teacher is one of the most powerful areas to think through. There are some labels that come easily – the age group you teach, the subject(s) within which you work, perhaps the type of school or area that you teach in. These are probably the answers you would give to someone in a social situation who asked you about your job, but there are also deeper answers – answers which reflect on the purpose you find in teaching and the approaches that you take to it. Whilst the first set of answers may come quickly, these deeper responses often do not. Despite the fact they shape every decision you make and every interaction you have with your classes, they are often left unsaid and largely not thought about explicitly.

We all have lenses through which we see the world. These lenses are shaped by many things, and often they differ depending on the context. We choose our lenses depending on how we want to operate, although this may not always be a conscious action. Our lenses are first shaped by our family experiences, and frequently this is the strongest influence affecting things like our values and morals. Our lenses are then further shaped by our schooling, again in terms of values but also by the subjects we study and the approaches within which we learn.

We tend to think mostly about the specific knowledge and skills that each subject we study gives us, but each subject also informs us about different ways of looking at the world. Sometimes this is explicit. For example, when studying literature or drama it would be quite normal to discuss in detail the perspectives of characters or writers and their motivations for behaving or communicating in the way they do. There is a lens being developed here also that is more implicit – that looking at the world through the eyes of others and considering their perspectives is something that we should do because it gives us better insight into the world. Some people take on and develop this lens more than others, just as some people continue to learn about a subject due to aptitude or interest.

Learning about mathematics and science provide knowledge about how certain aspects of the world work and the skills to manipulate these domains, but it also implicitly teaches a certain way of seeing. This lens reveals the underlying logic of the universe, a belief that there is one true explanation for things – if only we can find it – and that the only reason we cannot is that we are not always able to control for all of the complex variables that affect us.

Quite apart from merely being convenient boundaries for certain sets of knowledge or skills, the different subjects which we have come to study in school are based on particular ways of seeing the world, and the way we see the world is therefore affected by the degree to which we take these on and develop our thinking around them. There is, of course, a certain flexibility in this; depending on the type of situation we are presented with we are more likely to use certain lenses and not others. In situations where time is of the essence, deploying our philosophical lens and questioning every assumption involved in a decision will likely prevent that decision ever being made. At such times, seeing the world through a pragmatic lens – and accepting that whatever decision we make we will keep on moving forward – might be more appropriate.

By the time we come to be a teacher, we have already developed our own complex lenses that shape the way we understand what we do, our underlying purpose and approaches, and the way we make every decision in the classroom. My own intellectual lens has been significantly shaped by my study of history at university. I chose to specialise in exploring how scientific ideas have shaped social roles and how our understandings have affected our behaviour. This was particularly interesting to me because, when exploring this process in the past, we can see that the scientific ideas that we now think of as 'wrong' shaped the way people thought about various aspects of their lives and the world.

However, the lenses through which I see education have not only been shaped by these specifically academic influences, far from it. When I started teaching, I realised I was just as influenced by my own childhood when I was obsessed with making things. From early days with junk models, to making computer games and music studios, I have learnt a huge amount from my childhood projects. My appreciation for this learning outside the classroom has shaped the way I think about teaching as much as the subjects on the curriculum.

We all bring a range of experiences and learning to our own perspectives on teaching, and this, in turn, gives us all a unique perspective on how we see the purpose of schools and what we do in them. Paul Ernest characterises these perspectives as 'ideologies', which he describes as set of 'belief systems' with both an intellectual and a moral dimension.[1] Ideologies incorporate your perspective on knowledge and the nature of knowing, along with more moral and ethical dimensions, such as what you think the purpose of education is. Words such as 'moral' and 'ethical' tend to be loaded in everyday language. We often assume that there is just one perspective that is moral or one way of doing things that is purely ethical. In fact, people's morals and ethics are quite different, as are their ideologies. A difference in morals and ethics can be the source of major conflict in the staffroom and in international politics. However, few teachers define what their ideological position is explicitly. Many discussions I see and take part in become heated precisely because teachers are coming from very different ideological positions but not clearly articulating this all-important background to their arguments.

---

1 P. Ernest, *The Philosophy of Mathematics Education* (London: Routledge Falmer, 1991).

There is often the assumption that because we are teachers then our ideology must be the same. Perhaps this is because there are some broad positions that are likely to be quite similar for anyone deciding to commit themselves to a career in teaching. By its very nature, the job attracts individuals who want to make a difference to people's lives, who want to support and develop others, and who believe in the power of learning. However, these are broad brushstrokes and how you achieve those objectives, or even what success in achieving them looks like, is subject to huge differences in opinion. Ideologies in education are often about the details and the priorities that an individual gives to particular aspects of the broader aims.

These broad positions also bypass the most important question of all: why? We all might want to help develop young people's knowledge and skills, but our reasons for doing so can be quite diverse. For some teachers, the prime purpose of school is to prepare students for the world of work. Employers demand qualifications, and without them young people are unable to enter many careers; qualifications give them choices and opportunities. For others, the development of personal qualities and skills is the primary purpose of education. 'Rounded individuals' with a range of skills and a sense of who they are can become happy people who are able to both pursue their ambitions and deal with any setbacks. For other teachers, it is the study of academic disciplines that is important – instilling a love of study and learning and a thirst for figuring out how the world works from an analytical perspective. These are all simplistic caricatures, of course, but they demonstrate to some extent the huge variance in thinking on the purpose of education. There is little wonder that differences of opinion surface despite everyone being in it 'for the best for the children'.

Many of these ideological positions are very deep seated, and it takes enormous effort to shift your perspective and see the world through the eyes of someone with a different viewpoint, rather than just considering them as deluded or, even more problematically, assuming they think the same as you do. There are persuasive arguments for all of the positions outlined above, although with something as deep as this, logical argument does not always reveal the whole picture. These are not just intellectual positions, but emerge from morals, values and beliefs.

So, our ideologies are influenced by complex factors, but this is not to say that they are so complex as to not be worth defining. In order to have meaningful discussions we need to be able to create an understanding of where we are coming from, and this is often achieved by giving a name and a precise definition to the ideas to which different people subscribe. To use the words of the philosopher Anthony Grayling, 'clarity of language is clarity of thought';[2] to think clearly about things and to discuss them meaningfully we have to give them a clear definition.

Whenever I consider this concept, I am taken back to a staff meeting at a school where I was teaching once where we were discussing next steps for teaching and learning. I will never forget having a heated debate with a colleague about 'working walls' and whether they were useful. This went on for some time before we realised that they were talking about displays with prompts of vocabulary, facts and reminders of processes the children had learnt, and I was talking about displays created by children during the course of a topic including their ideas, rough work and emerging learning. Both are potentially useful approaches, but they are clearly quite different; not defining what we actually meant by the jargon meant we were talking at cross-purposes.

Clarity is important in any discussion or debate, and being clear about your ideology of education, and the ideology of your colleagues, helps hugely in understanding where people are coming from and the real implications of what they are saying. You do not have to agree with them, but trying to understand helps enormously in avoiding the

---

2 Quoted in O. Quinlan, Definition, Attribution and 'The Field', *Oliver Quinlan* (29 June 2012). Available at: www.oliverquinlan.com/blog/2012/06/29/definition-attribution-the-field/.

kinds of unproductive misunderstandings evidenced by my 'working walls' experience.

John Dewey described ideologies in education as either being 'traditionalist' or 'progressive'.[3] He characterised traditionalists as seeing education as the transmission of a body of knowledge and skills formulated in the past and communicated to young people in an institution that is separate from the society in which they are being prepared to participate. Progressives were characterised by Dewey as being more interested in expression, the cultivation of individuality and interacting with the world in a way that prepares young people for participation in a changing world by taking part in it. He summarised the two positions as the contrast between seeing education as an imposition from the outside and bringing out what is on the inside. In Dewey's analysis, we have two broad positions which would result in quite different outcomes in a classroom in terms of how lessons are constructed, what questions are asked and what interactions take place.

The inherent problem with language is that it can be both misconstrued, as some words have particular connotations for some of us and not others, and words can be used interchangeably in quite different circumstances. The word 'traditional' is used in a wide variety of contexts, but it is important to differentiate the ideology of 'Traditionalism' from the broader idea of being 'traditional'. If being traditional is defined as a situation being left unchanged from its original form, the most traditional of all approaches to learning would be arguably children growing up learning solely from their own families; however, this is far from a 'traditionalist' approach to education.

Another, more contemporary, set of positions emerge in the debate that often surfaces between the importance of learning knowledge versus acquiring skills or dispositions. Some would argue that this is only a new

---

3 J. Dewey, *Experience and Education* (New York: Free Press, 2007 [1938]).

and perhaps simplified expression of Dewey's views; others that it is an important distinction given the role technology is playing in redefining the role of knowledge. Few would maintain that *either* knowledge *or* skills should be taught exclusively in schools, but most teachers adopt a position somewhere on the continuum between these two standpoints. To see these as opposing concepts is a huge simplification, but it does help us to conceptualise our views and consider how our lessons contribute to their development. So, this can be a useful model if used to clarify our thinking, but not if it is seen as the way things actually are. As with any model, we must be willing to step outside of it when it is no longer useful.

Other ideological positions emerge from differences in our ideas about what knowledge is – our epistemology. The more straightforward view is that there are such things as 'facts' and 'truth', which can be confirmed and taught and understood as being 'right'. A more postmodern perspective would be that 'truth' is ethereal, that all knowledge is simply an interpretation or a perception and cannot be separated from the person or the conditions in which it arose. Where you stand on this debate might be affected by the disciplines that have influenced you in your studies; some areas of the sciences can tend towards the acceptance of universal truth, whilst others are inherently more accepting of an interpretive approach. In practice, we often find ourselves switching between the two depending on what we are considering. Although taking on a 'working acceptance' of one position or the other to best fit the circumstances can be useful, it is helpful to think about how you would define your own beliefs and philosophy.

We like to think in opposites or dichotomies and represent them in a 'for' or 'against' manner. The political left and right, knowledge and skills, fair and unfair, right and wrong; thinking in binary states comes easily to us. Perhaps this mirrors the many binary states that we experience in life: alive or dead, male or female, child or adult. It may be the case that we crave simplification to help us consider complex issues, but in reality, few things are rarely this simple. Whilst models such as this can be useful, it must be remembered that they are explanatory rather than prescriptive, and although they might help us to understand complex situations this does not reduce their complexity.

The left and right in politics is an obvious example of this, but some have argued that rather than a straight line this is better represented by Jean-Pierre Faye's horseshoe model. His theory takes the familiar linear left–right continuum and bends it into a horseshoe shape, with the extreme right and extreme left ending up very close together. The argument is that the experience of ordinary people in a regime run by either the extreme left or the extreme right is not hugely different; the citizens of Stalinist Russia and Nazi Germany had lives that were more similar than the dogma of their governments might have suggested.

The horseshoe theory privileges the experience of the people it affects rather than the political ideology, which could give us a different perspective on some models of educational ideology. If we were to put the traditionalist and progressive models onto a horseshoe and consider the experience of children learning under them, would the extremes actually look quite similar? It seems clear that the classrooms and the activities happening in them would differ, but in terms of the learning happening they may look quite alike. Critiques of extreme traditionalism might assert that little learning takes place when subjects and content are placed before the needs or interests of children; those of extreme progressivism might argue that when everything is left to emerge from the child they can never know what they don't know, and in constructing everything for themselves they miss out on the shortcuts to understanding and knowledge that have been developed over hundreds of years.

What emerges from considering ideologies via the horseshoe model is an argument for balance. The idea that radical positions are bad and balance is preferable is baked into the model. This produces another strong argument for being wary of models, as they can contain inherent arguments in the way that they are constructed.

In *The Philosophy of Mathematics Education*, Ernest paints a more complicated picture of educational ideologies as belonging to five broad groups which are defined as much by their political positions and historical roots as their specific ideas on education.[4] My colleague, Pete Kelly, has adopted this framework because, by including political dimensions, it helps to demonstrate the power relationships inherent in any ideology.

The model splits education ideologies into five distinct characters, although Ernest emphasises that, in reality, people may share a number aspects. The *industrial trainers* take a back-to-basics view of instilling children with core skills and social norms from an authoritarian view-point. The *technological pragmatists* take an objective-driven view of learning to provide children with useful skills and knowledge for the workplace. For the *old humanists*, academic learning is an aim in itself; a case of inducting young people into educated society. The *progressive educators* shift the focus from education as an external body of knowledge and skills to be learned, to something that is within a child and should be brought out or constructed through experimentation and play. For the *public educators*, the purpose of education is more about social mobility and social justice, and therefore centres on the development of questioning through authentic learning situations.

One of the distinctive features of this model is that it is quite explicit about the origins of each of these positions, and their resulting political links. When considering one's own ideology it is worth reflecting on where it comes from. Everyone has a unique background and history which will shape their belief systems, whether this is the circumstances in which they grew up, the jobs their parents did or particular life

---

4 Ernest, *The Philosophy of Mathematics Education*.

experiences they have had. Ideological positions are rarely far removed from this context. How has your background influenced your educational ideology?

The purpose of this chapter has been to consider the vast range of educational ideologies that exist, and explore the importance of considering and defining your own ideology. This is crucial for clarity with others when discussing education, but more importantly for clarity with yourself. Hopefully, the examples and discussion have prompted some thoughts about your own views about education and where you stand on some of these issues. Our positions change as we learn and experience new things, so the act of deeply considering these concepts may result in a realisation that the arguments we might have put forward in the past are flawed or need nuancing.

I am not arguing for a particular ideology here, but I am suggesting that we should all have one, which of course we do, and that it is worth the time and effort to consider this deeply and define clearly to ourselves what we actually think. For the thinking teacher clarity matters, for it is your ideology that shapes everything you do.

Chapter 3

The futility of utility

Debates around teaching and learning often have two main themes: what young people should be taught and how this teaching should happen. More often, it seems to be the latter that is the subject of discussion, largely because curricula are often defined and set centrally, whether by local or national governments or by those responsible for exams and certification; individual teachers often have little control over this. The decisions taken each day by teachers are primarily concerned with *how* they will be teaching rather than *what*, so this is an area of profound concern and dialogue.

At the time of writing, the debate in the UK is unusually focused on the what rather than the how, with the coalition government in the process of defining a completely new national curriculum. This is bringing out some interesting discussions about what children should be taught, not least the usefulness of subjects and their content.

The argument goes that what children learn in school should be useful, meaning that it should have a direct application in their lives. This is a perspective that is quite often expressed when people describe their own time at school. On the face of it, it seems to have some logic, but it is frequently problematic in practice.

Some knowledge and skills taught in schools are directly useful to most people's everyday lives. Basic written and spoken language allows us to communicate socially and in the workplace; numeracy is necessary to deal with money, measures and any number of everyday tasks. There are also many areas of the curriculum which are not used on a daily basis by many people – solving simultaneous equations is a good example. I am sure many adults will have not done this since they were last asked to do so during a maths lesson at school.

The difficulty comes when you consider that different people find practical applications for very different things in their lives. As a profession, teaching is very much based on interpersonal communication and relationships; it is not inherently a technical job unless you teach a technical subject. I spoke to an engineer recently about the simultaneous equations example, and he replied that the understanding and methods involved in this were in fact fundamental to what he does. He judged that he used simultaneous equations almost every day of his working life.

Therein lies the problem: what is useful on a day-to-day basis for a teacher is very different to what is useful for an engineer; to what is useful for any number of people in different jobs. The problem with focusing on what is useful in this way is that we risk restricting children to expectations based only on our own experiences. Even if we aim to teach only what will be useful to them in the future, we need to make sure that we consider *all* of their possible futures – and they may well go on to live very different lives to our own.

Ask a class of young children the classic question of what they want to be when they grow up, and you tend to get a large proportion of answers of either a teacher or whatever the children's parents do as a job. A large number of them imagine futures based only on what they know, and unless someone opens them up to a range of possibilities to aspire to, and the foundations to begin to get them there, then their aspirations could potentially be limited. It is interesting that this question is almost always met with a job title; we are often so focused on usefulness and application that when asked to define their future, children understand the question to be exclusively about a job.

A conflict is often depicted between learning things 'just in case' they are needed or 'just in time' for them to be useful. Just in time learning can be very powerful; learning something due to necessity makes it authentic and often highly engaging. It also helps develop the kind of lifelong learning skills that allow people to be adaptable, flexible and successful in a changing world.

Just in case learning is characterised as being less relevant and engaging; it lacks the immediate usefulness apparent when learning things because you need to use them there and then. Yet without it, much just in time learning can fall flat. If you are undertaking a project and you need to learn something new, the process can stall very quickly if you believe what you have to learn is too ambitious. If it is something small that can be built onto what you already know and can do, then extending your skills or knowledge in this way can be very approachable. If the required learning stops you proceeding with the task for a significant amount of time, then many of the benefits of learning in situ can be lost and it can become difficult to keep the momentum of the project going.

Some just in case learning is therefore needed to facilitate any just in time learning; some things just have to be mastered before they can become useful. As Carl Sagan famously said, 'If you wish to make an apple pie from scratch, you must first invent the universe.'[1] The problem is that if people are to undertake any work that is genuinely authentic, just as their own paths through life will be, it is impossible for teachers to teach them only the things they will definitely find useful. We can teach some of the more fundamental things with certainty, but we can never know about them all. We therefore need to teach some things that are not immediately useful, or that may never have been useful to us personally, in order that they find a use later, or at least create the opportunity for them to become useful.

---

1 C. Sagan, *Cosmos* (New York: Random House, 1980), p. 218.

With so much of our education system geared towards tangible out-comes such as grades, exam certificates and jobs, it is easy to forget that learning things that are useful and have a direct application is just one possible aim. Learning about art is not ostensibly useful unless one is to become an artist or work in the creative industries, yet without individuals outside of these spheres who have an appreciation of art such industries would not exist. The arts is the most obvious example, but the same is true for the sciences or any other subject; it is beneficial to learn about things we will never directly apply for the simple reason that it helps us to appreciate and understand the world that we live in, and ourselves. In all the discussion of what would be useful for young people to learn in school, we must not forget that we often gain the most from that which has the least practical use, for it is this that encourages us to think.

Chapter 4
Technology as a mirror

We live in radically changing times, so the popular sayings go, and much of that change is down to technology. I have lost count of the number of conference speeches I have seen showing the *Shift Happens* video, wowing those watching with the huge numbers of highly educated people coming out of economically emerging areas such as India and China, or the fact that the top ten in-demand jobs in 2010 did not exist in 2004, or that the pace of technological change is resulting in the volume of data we store doubling every two years. Vast increases in communications, information and our ingenuity make technology a seductive force in our lives. It is easy to paint technology as being the answer to everything, but it is worth exploring what role it really plays in our lives, and therefore what role it should play in the learning of young people.

Technological skills are more important than ever to successfully navigate our way in the world. In many disciplines this has been the case for some time. Science, engineering and the new fields of digital media quite obviously require technological skills, but increasingly, even less specialist and more traditional jobs have integrated technology to a significant degree. A job in retail now requires the use of complex point-of-sale systems in customer-facing roles, whilst inventory and stock-taking systems are commonplace in warehouses. Farming is also driven by specialist technologies, from global positioning systems in tractors to sophisticated electronic tagging systems for produce. Administration in all fields has increasingly been taken over by time-saving technologies, often replacing the human administrators and secretaries who used to do such jobs, but thereby requiring everyone else to learn how to interface with and use these new systems.

To get and keep a job, young people need expertise with new technologies. However, suggesting that they should learn these skills at school is more contentious. Almost all young people now grow up using devices that require them to develop this know-how, and the design of new media is undertaken with a significant focus on making them as easy to use as possible. Another education technology conference favourite is one of the many videos of babies confidently navigating their way around an iPad; it is not unusual to find even primary school children who are more confident at using new technology than their teachers. However, there are many people effectively operating in a world of work saturated with digital technologies who never had access to them at school and who learned how to use them later in life. All of these factors make the argument that schools need to teach children how to use technology to survive in the modern world a problematic one; they are already doing so in many situations that have nothing to do with school.

At one time, it was seen as sensible for schools to teach generic 'IT skills' as a separate subject, but many have now moved towards the understanding that, just as in the world outside school, technology is most effective when used as a means to an end. The integration of mobile technology into schools mirrors how it is used in the wider world, allowing it to be used in ways that can support or enhance the learning. The problem is that for this to work, technology needs to be designed and implemented in ways that will have an impact on the learning, not merely for the sake of it. Taking into account the way technology has so naturally become a central part of our world, and given the drive to use it as an integrated tool for other things, it would be easy to surmise that it is enough to simply create access to a range of devices and allow its use to develop. Often new technologies have been depicted as the silver bullet that will enhance learning by merely being present in a classroom, and money has been spent on putting them there in the hope that they will seamlessly integrate into the learning experience as easily and transparently as mobile phones and social networks have integrated into our lives.

New media technologies have seemingly crept into our social lives, but this is because they have been very carefully designed for this purpose – at great expense and with great expertise. Facebook has been specifically engineered as a suite of tools to make social communications easy, mimicking the way social behaviours work in the real world, enhancing them with the power of long-distance communication, and encouraging more connections and sharing by augmenting these processes and speeding them up. Much of the new technology we see being put into schools has not been designed with anything like this degree of focus on the kinds of specific behaviours that happen in classrooms, and even if this has been taken into account, often the focus has been on behaviours that are not as beneficial for learning as they might be.

A classic example of this is the proliferation of interactive whiteboards (IWBs). Since the early 2000s, a large amount of money has been spent on installing IWBs in classrooms across the UK – many schools now have one in every classroom. IWBs were seen as the next stage in teaching technology – that better presentation tools and more inter-activity in classrooms would increase student engagement in learning. In London, every school received funding for IWBs and the results were evaluated by Professor Dylan Wiliam.[1] However, he found that the initiative had no discernible impact on the achievement of learners, and in some schools there was actually evidence of achievement going down after they were introduced.

The reasons for this are complex, but one factor worth considering is the design of the IWB and how this affects the way they are used. Whilst the touch-based technology they use allowed interaction with the projected display of a computer, they were still a single focus-point installed at the front of a classroom and, as such, they were often used with an entire class at once. There was interactivity for the teacher and one or

---

1 D. Wiliam, Assessment, Learning and Technology: Prospects at the Periphery of Control. Keynote speech at the Association for Learning Technology Conference in Nottingham (2007). Available at: www.scribd.com/doc/44566598/null.

two students at the front of the classroom, but this did not necessarily extend to the rest of the students. Unless the teacher moved their focus off the technology and towards more low-tech interactivity for all, such as discussion or the use of mini whiteboards (or even paper!), lessons were unchanged for most of the pupils for most of the time.

Although IWBs have now moved on, the original technology only allowed for one person to operate them at a time – the irony being that a teacher could introduce more interactivity into their lessons by asking every student to do something on a piece of paper than by using the board. At a time when educational thinking was turning towards person-alisation and formative assessment, IWBs, in some senses, reinforced a teacher-led and didactic approach to teaching and learning. It must be acknowledged that many teachers recognised this and sought to avoid it, making effective use of IWBs as just one tool at their disposal to facilitate different types of learning. However, Wiliam's research shows that this was often not the case, and IWBs are still being marketed as a tool for teacher-directed learning rather than real interactivity. We can-not get away from the fact that this is how they were originally designed and, therefore, IWBs often reinforce a type of teaching which paradoxi-cally lacks interactivity.

More recently, lower costs have meant that sophisticated technology such as laptops and tablet computers are now available to many schools. Equipping a class with a sufficient number of these devices, and com-mitting to using them, is likely to encourage the designing of lessons built around more student interaction. However, it must be remembered that these devices have not been designed with learning in mind. This is not inherently good or bad, but it is certainly useful to consider how this affects the ways in which teachers deploy them in the classroom.

Take as an example the iPad, in which increasing numbers of schools are investing. As well as being a very seductive new technology, iPads also seem like a good deal financially: it is very difficult to find a capable laptop at the same price point and certainly not one with the same slick design and aesthetic appeal. However, the mistake is to think of iPads as having been designed as laptop replacements. The iPad has been conceived specifically as a personal mobile device. From the fact that it has no system for logging in different users, to the way it stores the password for your email account, it has been designed to be used by one person exclusively. Schools that have accepted this fact and deployed iPads accordingly – purchasing or subsidising one that is 'owned' by each learner – are finding that this leads them to different ways of working than they would have with traditional laptops, which were usually owned by schools and given out at the start of lessons. When students have their own device, many new ways of working can emerge, not least using them for one small part of a lesson, when appropriate, and not the all-consuming lesson where all activities revolve around them.

Many schools are still purchasing iPads as laptop replacements and then finding that they are simply unsuited to being stored in trolleys of fifteen devices that are used by multiple people a day. Those schools that are managing to make this work are thinking very carefully about the ways in which the devices are designed and how they can work around this, or embrace it. Some are focusing on the immediate access to the web that they provide and encouraging teachers to build research activities into their teaching; others are making use of the integrated cameras which allow them to be used for planning, shooting, editing and publishing multimedia presentations and films. The important point is they are considering how iPads are designed and how teachers want to construct learning, and then making the two fit together. Not considering the second of these, and simply putting technology into classrooms because of a vague sense that schools should be using the latest tools, is a fairly good way of ensuring that it will not be used effectively for learning or even become a distraction from it.

There is, however, an underlying issue with deploying new computer technologies in schools: buying into consumer technology involves a school buying into, and in some senses promoting, the consumer culture for which they have been designed. Devices designed deliberately to be tied to one person may provide convenience, but they also conveniently (for the manufacturers) mean we all have to buy our own. Consumer technologies are also increasingly designed in such a way that they have a short life, with some manufacturers tending towards batteries that are not removable and hence not replaceable when they fail. Some devices are also so stylised in their construction that they cannot be repaired but must be replaced if damaged. This raises important questions about sustainability and environmental impact. The technology we choose is in some senses a political choice as well as a practical one, and there are ethical issues around inducting young people in our consumer culture without encouraging them to question and challenge it.

Implementing technology transparently is about making it so fitted into the day-to-day learning that it ceases to be exciting. Unfortunately, historically, the limited access to technology in schools has ensured that it has always been an exciting event when the students actually get to use it. Whilst the schools using technology most effectively might be making it transparent, what is more interesting is what is made visible when this happens.

My colleague Pete Yeomans uses a wonderfully illustrative slide when discussing the use of new technologies in schools showing a canoe made of transparent Perspex floating in a tropical ocean. I know little about boat-building, but I imagine that boat builders could get excited about the innovative construction of such a craft, much as technophiles do about the latest gadget. For the rest of us, what is more exciting about such a boat is not that it is transparent, but that it allows us to see the sea and fish below. Such is also the case with new technologies; it is not the technologies themselves that are most interesting, but what is made visible when they are transparently integrated into our lives.

A prime example of issues being made visible by technology is the debate around the use of search engines and the abundance of information available on the web. The availability of information since the widespread adoption of internet access has clearly had an effect on learning and schools. Where once school libraries and textbook collections provided access to a certain amount of knowledge, this has increased astronomically, with information on almost any subject available at the click of a button or, increasingly, the touch of a screen.

This has led to some educationalists arguing that the acquiring of knowledge is no longer as important as it once was. Knowledge used to be scarce, to be studiously built up just in case you needed it. This argument is often made by emphasising the by-rote memorising of knowledge practised in traditional schools, complete with blackboards and rows of children reciting times tables. Now, so the reasoning goes, facts and knowledge can be easily found in seconds using the phone in your pocket. With a hotline to everything the human race has ever known, what has now become important is not knowing things, but knowing how and where to find them – the skills of searching rather than the discipline of memorising.

This is a seductive argument for many reasons, in no small part because memorising and remembering things is hard work. Most of us can recollect learning our times tables or musical scales. It takes considerable time and effort and often is not very interesting. Teachers can set up ways to frame memorisation as being more attention-grabbing by introducing novelty into the process, but ultimately the whole purpose of the exercise is the reverse of novelty – a whole lot of repetition. Memorising has therefore developed a bad reputation, particularly with the increasing emphasis on making learning in school exciting and engaging, as well as the fact that remembering activities generally do not take much effort to set up. This has led to some teachers avoiding memorisation tasks in lessons.

Despite the almost instantaneous access to knowledge that the internet affords us, knowing some facts is still very important in many situations. To take the example of musical scales, this information can be very easily looked up online. A quick search of Wikipedia can tell me what notes are in the scale of A minor, and if I was trying to compose a piece of music with my computer and keyboard, this would be of great help. I can take as long as I like trying notes on the keyboard until I find something that sounds pleasant, or I can draw them on screen in different orders until the computer is playing a melody I like. What Wikipedia completely fails to tell me, though, is what A minor *feels* like. I can flick back and forth between windows, checking what notes are in the scale and trying them out in my composition, but I cannot really play the scale and improvise with it unless I have learnt it. Moreover, I could have done exactly the same thing with a book of scales. The delivery mechanism of the web means I can get hold of this information much faster, but the way I use it is no different unless I actually learn it.

Without knowing about a few more scales, I also could not have made a decision about which scale to use based on the feelings I want to express, and would be left choosing from whatever limited selection I already know about, or googling 'what scale to use to be sad', which is a very different process of self-expression. In the same way, it is also difficult to improvise with a group of people without knowing what keys to play in. Consequently, the rather cold and dry process of memorisation is actually extremely important for expressing emotions and being able to do so in the moment. I write this as someone with a good understanding of how musical notation works but no knowledge of scales; as someone who has been able to compose music on a computer but completely failed to play any of it live. Whilst I may possess many skills in music production, I simply do not know enough to perform my music or to jam with other people and express myself in a group situation.

A similar situation arises with times tables — surely one of the most straightforward pieces of information to look up on the internet. I can click the search button on my computer screen, type in a multiplication and it will tell me the answer. Everyone has access to a calculator almost instantly these days: you can use Google, Excel or the calculator on your phone. But I think many people would agree that this is no substitute for knowing your times tables. It may be interesting for us to consider why this is the case.

Firstly, there is speed: knowing your times tables is always quicker than the quickest device that can do it for you. Secondly, there is the practicality of freeing you from needing the device. Since the advent of calculators in the 1980s, people have argued about practicality, although with the increasing ubiquity of devices with calculator functions this is becoming less relevant. But speed will not be beaten until we have a computer interface to which we can issue commands and receive a response as fast as we can think. However, the more compelling point is that knowing your times tables changes the way you think. With technology you can look up the answer to a specific problem when it is explicitly posed to you, but when you know your tables off by heart you are able to notice patterns in other scenarios in ways that you are highly unlikely to do without this knowledge. If you know your times tables you can spot that a problem solved using a multiple of eight can also be solved using a multiple of four, or that certain lengths convert more straightforwardly between inches and centimetres, or work much more quickly with problems where you have an answer but need to work back to discover elements in the question.

The examples used here are about basic skills, because these most clearly illustrate the argument, but the same holds true for more complex bodies of knowledge. Knowing more about scientific concepts allows you to make links and predictions based on their relationships – for example, the way light and sound work is based on similar principles, so a solid knowledge of one significantly aids understanding of the other. The more knowledge you have about historical events or narrative structures, the wider your range of interpretations of history or literature.

Clearly, there is a limit to what you can know and remember, and there are many things relating to your interests or your job that you do not need to actually memorise. For those matters, the ubiquity of devices connected to the web makes things quicker and easier. Until we have Amazon-like recommendation engines in our heads, stating 'people who thought about ... also found it useful to think about ...', the internet will not replace the way that knowing things helps you to think, but rather augment it.

The proliferation of information has undoubtedly changed the way we learn and access it, but knowledge is still as important as it has ever been, albeit in subtly different ways. This may seemingly lead the debate right back to the start, but having considered these issues and their subtleties makes us appreciate their complexities more. When there was no alternative to memorising information to build up knowledge, the need to question the complexity of the importance of knowledge was less obvious. Presented with the challenge of the web, we are forced to consider how we interact with knowledge more deeply and, as a result, this brings us to a greater appreciation of the importance of some things that many of us took for granted in the past.

To return to the analogy of the transparent boat, it is not the transparency of the boat that matters but what it makes visible. Boats have always operated by floating above a great body of water, cruising over all manner of interesting creatures and habitats beneath the surface. The transparent boat does exactly the same, but it makes its occupants more aware of how they are interacting with the world in ways that reveal more about that world and about themselves. By externalising this perspective, teachers can think about the way learners approach their interactions with knowledge and skills; it also makes learners think about how they are learning. Technology can be a great tool, but for teachers it can also reveal the thinking we have already and the thinking that we might develop about learning.

Chapter 5
Quantifying learning

In 1988, the band The KLF published a book called *The Manual*, a systematic, step-by-step guide on how to have a number one single with no financial backing and no musical talent.[1] *The Manual*, and the counterpart number one single they released as The Timelords, demonstrate the powerful potential of quantifying and systematising something in order to communicate and learn it, an area in which there are currently some fascinating developments.

We often like to believe that art and music are based on emotion, that there is something pure in the way they communicate to us. Bill Drummond and Jimmy Cauty subverted this with *The Manual* by setting out a systematic method for achieving a number one single, backed by their extensive experience in the music industry and the fact they had created a number one record using exactly the same methods. The book details every action they took in creating and marketing their record, 'Doctorin' the Tardis', from educating the reader about the processes used in recording studios right down to describing how to deceive a bank manager into funding such a venture. The book itself was clearly intended as a subversive joke, an opportunity to poke fun at how the music industry in the late 1980s worked, but there are a number of documented cases of bands taking their advice at face value and precisely emulating their success to produce their own number one records. Many other successful artists also cite its influence on them. This raises some interesting questions as to how far we can quantify and emulate a complex and emotive process such as producing music.

---

1 B. Drummond and J. Cauty, *The Manual (How To Have a Number One the Easy Way)* (n.p.: KLF Publications, 1988). The book is now out of print but it is available online at: www.kirps.com/web/main/resources/music/themanual/.

As teachers, I think we often have a difficult relationship with quantifying and systematising what happens in classrooms. On one level we know that learning is a process full of mystery, that young people are unique and capable of producing huge surprises, but on another we inhabit a system in which measuring, labelling and tracking are given great importance. We often feel that these quantifying forces are imposed on us externally, whether by managers, Ofsted inspectors or government initiatives. This can lead to a sense of needing to redress the balance by making sure that those areas not touched by the system remain free, open and mysterious. However, there is also a case for exploring how learning is measured and how this can be used to enable and encourage it to happen, rather than something that gets in its way.

Design Thinking consultant Ewan McIntosh often presents insights from the creative industries to teachers. His work with creatives shows that far from being completely free-flowing in what they do, many of them have strong systems and processes in place to support creativity as a repeatable process rather than the outcome of uncontrolled flashes of inspiration. In 2012, McIntosh shared a useful model from the design business for thinking about how we consider systematising in learning and teaching.[2] He took Roger Martin's 'knowledge funnel',[3] a model designed for thinking about the tension between innovation and systems in business, and considered how it applies to teachers.

Martin's model consists of three stages that ideas go through to be implemented successfully on a large scale: mystery, heuristics and algorithms. According to the model, ideas start out buried in mystery – we don't know what is happening or what will work. If someone comes up with an idea, planting a flag in this ocean of possibilities, sometimes it will work if the conditions are right; but as there is little understanding

---

2 E. McIntosh, SSAT National Conference: Keynote 12 (7 December 2012) [video]. Available at: www.youtube.com/watch?v=vxep72WxQSA.

3 R. Martin, *The Design of Business: Why Design Thinking is the Next Competitive Advantage* (Boston, MA: Harvard Business School Publishing, 2009).

of why things work at this stage, many schemes will also fail when they are repeated. A very similar situation occurs in most people's learning when they are faced with a totally new area. One example is the process new teachers go through right at the start of their teaching practice. Often they are placed in a classroom with an experienced teacher and a lot of what is happening around them is a mystery. They see the teacher doing certain things that work, and when it comes to their turn to teach they will likely copy these techniques. At first this is often not underpinned by an understanding of why a certain technique is being used. However, with so much to learn, trainees begin by doing what works and gets results whether or not they understand why. This can frequently lead to techniques being applied at the wrong time or place, or in a way that misses a particular subtlety that was needed in this situation.

As people gain experience in an area, their ideas start to join up, bolstered by reflection and perhaps further study; simple actions begin to become rules of thumb. These patterns of things that work, and those that do not, become what Martin calls heuristics. These lead to a wider understanding and a set of rules that can be used to navigate a given area. McIntosh suggests that this is where much of teaching lies – as a set of adaptable heuristics that are used to make sense of the mystery of learning that is happening in a classroom.

The third stage of Martin's model is algorithms, or very specific sets of rules and actions that will yield results in any situation. These are not flexible understandings, but hard and fast instructions to be followed; frequently they have been designed to work successfully regardless of the context. Martin believes algorithms are the foundation for business practices that scale, such as the recipes and workflows in fast-food restaurants; wherever you are in the world, you can rely on getting much the same experience in a McDonald's as you would in your home town.

McIntosh observes that moving from mystery to heuristics is a recognisable process to teachers, yet there is something about the idea of teaching via algorithms that can be a difficult notion to accept. Teaching to rigid instructions, no matter how well designed, tends to jar with the concept we have of teachers as being adaptable, creative and able to fit our practice to the needs of our students. Teachers prize this professional freedom and guard it closely; it is a freedom which persists despite the presence of prescriptive curricula and accountability regimes. Sir Ken Robinson once commented on education systems: 'when the door closes … on your classroom, you are the education system so far as those kids are concerned'.[4] Despite feeling that teachers are under more scrutiny than ever, when it comes to the actions we take in our day-to-day practice, we still have a lot of freedom. Perhaps it is precisely this scrutiny that causes us to say the word 'algorithm' with such a bitter taste in our mouths. With all the pressures to carry out our jobs according to a formula, filling the areas we do have control over with prescribed systems seems unattractive.

Another reason that teachers can baulk at the idea of algorithms is that whilst operating in the area of mystery is very daunting at first, the buzz that individuals get from making things work in this situation is alluring. There is nothing quite like the sense of achievement you get when you pull something off despite not really knowing why. I was recently talking to a student who was recounting their experience of teaching English as a foreign language in the Far East. She had been expecting to shadow an experienced teacher for a while, having had only minimal training in the UK, but instead was thrown in at the deep end and asked to take a class. She said she was glad it had happened this way, as she managed to hold it together despite having no idea what she was doing, thereby learning a lot and feeling a massive sense of achievement. After a while, a friend who doesn't work in education asked the question that I was holding back for fear of being churlish: 'That's great, but who got the most out of this – you or the children?'

---

4 K. Robinson, with K. Facer, K. and M. Waters, Learning Without Frontiers [video] (16 March 2011). Available at: www.youtube.com/watch?v=-iL4rtDnfts.

There is a danger that if managing to last the day without chaos break-ing out feels like a great achievement, there could be little space left for significant learning. In situations like these, we are working so far away from what is perfect that *anything* we achieve is perceived as a great achievement, and consequently feels good. When it is possible to gain a sense of achievement from very little, the risk is that there is little impetus to up the stakes to realising a truly big achievement. I think this is part of the reason for teachers' resistance to systems or algorithms in their practice. In the world of mystery everything feels like a great achievement; in the world of heuristics and algorithms more is expected of us – the real wins are in improvements to well-established systems which are much harder to achieve. Working to heuristics and algorithms feels less rewarding than working to mystery.

This is apparent in other fields as well. Since the advent of digital tech-nology in music production, new styles of music have developed that are based more around the techniques of production than traditional playing. There is magic in mystery, at least in the feelings you get when you obtain results from this approach. Whether the results are really novel is harder to tell.

Some difficult professional ethics also come into play. A musician might opt to avoid algorithms and rules in their practice, but they do not have a responsibility to other people. If the album they spend a year on fails to be a hit, it might impact on the enjoyment of their fans, the record company's profits and perhaps their own livelihood. If a teacher fails, then they fail in their responsibility to a significant number of young people who never get the chance to have that period of their education again.

Think back to the best teachers you remember. I would be willing to bet that for most people enthusiasm would be one of the defining factors that make a teacher memorable. We know that enthusiastic teach-ers connect with students and encourage them to achieve. However, knowing your subject inside out and just following the rules day after day is unlikely to lead to such enthusiasm. Conversely, shooting in the dark is likely to lead to much passion, but not necessarily practice that is as well thought through and as effective as it could be.

As teachers we create our own heuristics and algorithms in the way we teach. We all build up certain ways of doing things, some as approaches or general rules that are infinitely adaptable, but also some that are basically strict algorithms that are repeated time after time. Much advice on managing disruptive behaviour, for example, stresses the importance of having a sequence of consequences that will be applied in very clear and unchanging ways to ensure everyone knows exactly where they are. Many of us also develop algorithms for more positive uses – the things that are so well refined that they just work, such as a particular explanation for a tricky concept or provocative questions that always get a discussion going.

Much teacher training and continuing professional development (CPD) deal with the heuristics of teaching and learning rather than any distinct instructions. University-based initial teacher education courses spend a great deal of time looking at the purposes of education and understanding how people learn, rather than the specific actions of teachers (as does much CPD). We work with others to develop our understandings of the wider heuristics of teaching, but we work alone to develop our algorithms.

Research has been conducted into developing teaching using algorithm-like structures – for example, some of Dylan Wiliam's work on formative assessment techniques. His BBC2 television series, *The Classroom Experiment*, was an interesting case study into the use of algorithm-like instructions to improve the learning happening in classrooms. In particular, this concentrated on the implementation of his 'no hands up' technique – a simple but powerful way to shift the way questions and answers are used in a classroom. Rather than the teacher asking a question, waiting for volunteers to put their hands up and then choosing someone to answer, students never put their hands up. A question is posed, some thinking time given and then a student's name is chosen at random from a pot of sticks containing the names of the entire class.

The rationale behind this idea is that the first hands to go up are usually the students who already know the answer and haven't had to think. Those students who need some thinking time to reach an answer can rely on them to give it. The result is that nobody thinks. With the no hands up system, the individual required to answer could be anyone, so the theory is that everyone has to think in case they are picked. This has to be coupled with an expectation that responding with 'I don't know' is not acceptable, and that if selected, the student has to give some kind of answer, at the very least sharing their thinking even if an answer itself is not quite formulated. A second name can also be chosen at random and that student asked to respond to the first response and so on, thus ensuring that the thinking is spread around the class and not just left to those who already 'get it'.

I have tried the no hands up technique myself and found that, like the teachers in the television series, despite this being quite a simple idea, it was initially quite challenging to implement. Firstly, it goes against a lot of the ingrained behaviour for both teacher and students. Despite explaining the concept in detail, I found I still had hands going up, and a number of the children who were used to contributing the lion's share of the answers got frustrated that they were not being picked. Secondly, I became aware that I had a tendency to ask questions in order to involve the class in driving the lesson forward – and I knew which students would quickly furnish me with an answer – so the pace of lessons slowed right down. However, this made me realise that whilst superficially my previous technique had seemed to involve the children, it wasn't actually ensuring any thinking happened. It was much more efficient for me to move quickly through this information-giving and then spend more time asking questions that were actually challenging and required deep thinking. Using the no hands up technique at this point helped to spread the thinking around the class. Eventually, my questions shifted to being more appropriate and more intellectually challenging, and the class got used to being asked to think more regularly. In that sense it was a great success, but it was quite a challenge to change the algorithmic behaviours of both myself and the students.

The key reason this technique can be hard to implement is that in order to make it work some deeply ingrained habits have to be replaced. It might be useful to think about our habits as algorithms; after all, the specific things that we do all the time eventually become automatic. This has the benefit that we do them without thinking, but the drawback is that if they are not beneficial then we are often stuck with them, and it is difficult to break such established patterns. We should therefore reflect on the habits we have developed as teachers.

Habits can be constraining, but they can also be some of the most powerful things that we do. The word 'habit' is often accompanied by the word 'bad', bringing with it visions of biting fingernails, eating badly or smoking. Such habits are hard to break, precisely because they are things we do without really thinking about them. We quickly build routines in the classroom, and whilst we may consciously want to do things differently, making the change can be difficult. It is easy to forget that the power of habit can also be used for good. Perhaps when we feel we are doing things naturally all we've really done is internalised enough algorithms to be carrying them out automatically. In actual fact, that effortless flow we feel when we are in our element could mean that our mechanistic algorithms have become so deeply rooted that we no longer think about them.

Science fiction writer and blogger Cory Doctorow has elegantly summed up the potential power of habits. He says that the best advice he was ever given was to write every day because then 'it becomes a habit and you do it automatically', adding 'habits are things you get for free'.[5] Although making something into a habit can be difficult, once you have it is something you can do regularly without the mental hard work. As such, habits can be incredibly powerful and forming the right ones can make a huge difference to the way you teach. It is the things that you do repeatedly that often have the biggest effect in your classroom rather than the one-offs. Small things such as giving students more time to think when asking them questions or following a no hands up policy, as described above, can significantly alter the learning experience in your classroom when repeated day after day.

There are two crucial points to making something into a habit. The first is to make it as straightforward and repeatable as possible. Distilling what you want to do into a simple set of instructions has two benefits: it gets to the key of what the task is about and helps you to concentrate only on what truly matters; and the simpler it is to remember, the easier it is to perform as a habit.

The second point is also useful for breaking bad habits, and that is to put things in place to force a certain action or behaviour. Making a public commitment is a good way to do this, particularly a commitment to the students in your class as they are usually very good at reminding you if you go off track. Tell them that you are always going to give them ten seconds to consider the answer to any question you ask – they will soon tell you if you are dropping back into picking the individuals who knew the answer already to feed back. If they do not, then the guilt of realising you have stopped doing something you committed to might. Alternatively, think about what you could change to push yourself into a new habit or out of a bad one. If you realise you spend large amounts of time in one spot in the classroom and want to divide your attention more across the room, consider how you could reorganise your room. Moving your chair or desk or placing your computer in a different part of

---

5 Quoted in T. Miller, I'm Cory Doctorow and This Is How I Work, *Lifehacker* (4 March 2013). Available at: lifehacker.com/5993401/im-cory-doctorow-and-this-is-how-i-work.

the room to other resources you regularly need are simple changes that will compel you to move around and focus your attention on different parts of the room as you do so.

Changes do not have to be directly focused on the habit you want to make or break, as long as they result in forcing you in or out of it. Changes also need to be straightforward enough to become automatic, so that a trigger can result in the action you want. Habits are things we do without thinking, so make them clear-cut or turn them into algorithms you can internalise.

An interesting case study of an algorithmic approach to learning comes in the form of bestselling author Tim Ferris. Introducing Ferris is a challenge – it feels disingenuous to merely describe him as an author given that his accomplishments include being a champion martial artist, a successful competitive salsa dancer, a business investor and a writer of books giving unconventional perspectives on business, health and fitness and cookery. Ferris is someone who has done a wide variety of things to a very high level and his secret, which is made clear in his books, is systematising the way he learns.

In *The 4 Hour Work Week*, he sets out a specific set of algorithms for creating a business and optimising it to take up the smallest amount of time possible.[6] The method he describes involves eliminating as much decision-making as possible, as this is what takes up most time for business owners. Key to his method is testing, leaving something to run and then retesting the results. This approach means that actions are judged on their effectiveness after they have been carried out, rather than what they felt like at the time of the decision. So often we make decisions based on whether they feel right; Ferris advocates trying the decision out, testing it and then deciding whether it was right choice.

---

6 T. Ferris, *The 4 Hour Work Week: Escape 9–5, Live Anywhere and Join the New Rich* (New York: Random House, 2009).

When looking at classroom habits, we often miss some of the small but important things that we do. An 8-year-old in one of my classes once told me she had counted me saying 'OK' forty times whilst I was explaining and giving instructions in one lesson. I had no idea this verbal tick was happening, but for those listening it was understandably annoying, and had distracted her enough from the lesson to have counted them all. Filming or recording yourself teaching can be a powerful tool for gaining insights into your practice. It may feel strange at first as you see yourself in the way that others do, but this is precisely why it is valuable. The separation and objectivity that watching or listening to yourself brings will reveal any habits – the things you never even think about. Once revealed, they are ready to be changed; or you might find a few that are actually quite positive but you didn't have the chance to appreciate them before.

Ferris's systematised approach clearly evolved from his understanding of business, but he has gone on to apply it to learning. Rather than asking people how they do things, his approach is to observe, test and then replicate, which has led to some surprising results. For example, his health and fitness book, *The 4 Hour Body*, is filled with unconventional but apparently effective approaches to eating and exercise that have been developed by watching what people actually do, trying it out and then testing it.[7] Everything is distilled into an algorithm with a particular purpose, but importantly the approach also involves testing the algorithm to make sure it is having the desired effect.

As Ferris acknowledges, learning to master something takes years. However, he bases his learning approaches on the Pareto principle – the idea that, in many situations, eighty per cent of the effects come from twenty per cent of the causes. His approach is to identify and learn the twenty per cent of skills or knowledge that create the positive results in eighty per cent of cases. Becoming a master of something takes more

---

7 T. Ferris, *The 4 Hour Body: An Uncommon Guide to Fat Weight Loss, Incredible Sex and Becoming Superhuman* (London: Vermilion, 2011).

than eighty per cent, but being eighty per cent usually makes you proficient. The challenge is in quantifying and defining what is the twenty per cent that you need to learn to get to that point.

Ferris's approach is very analytical, and involves making some quite stark decisions about what to learn and what not to learn, with a constant focus on desired outcomes and what is necessary to achieve them. Such is the requirement when devising specific algorithms for learning a new skill. Whilst this method may appear restrictive, his argument is that by being ruthless with these definitions you can achieve goals quickly, leaving time and space to accomplish other things.

As with everything, great teaching is not as simple as choosing between following algorithms, working with heuristics or sticking to mystery. What is important is to consider where and how we are using these levels and what effects this is having. Too much mystery and we run the risk of stabbing in the dark, not really knowing what works and what doesn't. Too many algorithms and we lose our enthusiasm and with it that of our students, or we can apply the wrong approaches without really thinking. Heuristics seem like a good middle ground, but again, considering deeply everything we do leaves little time for the doing; there is a balance to be struck.

The nuances of this problem are exemplified by my colleague Alexis Kirke, a computer music researcher with two doctorates, one in music composition and the other in computing. When discussing different approaches to research he told me that, since completing his PhDs, he now concentrates on the technical computer science side for his academic research rather than the creative composition side. His reasoning is that the perspective he needs for research is detachment, of leaving no stone unturned until he understands every aspect. For him, this clinical approach works well for the way he thinks about computer science; but in terms of composition, he tells me he wants to maintain his creative outlook of being excited and surprised, of being able to work partly through happy accidents.

The KLF's book was published in the late 1980s, and no one has claimed to have a number one single using it for quite some years; in fact, the very meaning of having a number one single has changed considerably now that downloads, YouTube videos and music streaming constitute so much of the music we listen to. Drummond and Cauty's algorithmic approach may have brought success a few decades ago, but now *The Manual* reads more like an interesting chronicle of the music industry of that time. Our culture has changed considerably in the past few decades and many of the instructions appear dated and refer to what is now antiquated technology and forgotten cultural details. Therein lies the problem with algorithmic approaches to anything; the more specific they are, the more closely things can be replicated, but the less flexible they are to change and the more liable they are to become out of date as things around them evolve.

Ultimately, systematisation works well for some things, others less so. What is important is that the benefits and drawbacks are considered and we make thoughtful choices about what to classify and what to leave looser in order to get the best out of ourselves and our students.

Chapter 6
Best practice or next practice?

The best way to predict the future is to invent it.

Alan Kay

If you wanted to get really good at something new, how would you approach it? One of the most obvious ways is to seek out someone who is regarded as an expert and learn what they do. This might be in person, by talking to them or watching them work, or if they have become well-known for what they do, perhaps listening to them speak at a conference or workshop. Some might have gained enough exposure to have written a book or created a website so many others can learn from them without even meeting them. Whether this process happens formally through reading a book or attending a course, or informally through asking a friend or colleague whose skills you admire to explain how they do it, seeking out those with the skills and learning from them is one of the most common ways to learn.

For many years, the teaching profession has been familiar with the term 'best practice'; sharing what is working well in one setting or for one teacher so that it might be implemented in another. This is the very essence of the 'teaching practice' models used in teacher education and training, whereby a new teacher spends time working alongside an experienced colleague, observing what they do and gradually taking over and implementing the teaching themselves. Both new and developing teachers are often encouraged to observe lessons taught by others so that they might take away techniques and strategies to implement in their own classrooms. This model also applies to INSETs where speakers are invited into schools to pass on what has worked for them in other schools, to conferences where presenters share best practice that they have carried out or that has worked successfully in other schools, and even to official publications from bodies such as Ofsted and government departments which communicate how the 'best' schools are doing things.

Some of the individuals sharing their formulae for best practice have done this so successfully that they have moved out of the classroom and established a new career working with schools to implement what they did so well in their own, and disseminating stories of success so that others might replicate it. This can sometimes raise tensions in training sessions because speakers sharing examples of good teaching practice can sometimes be subject to the criticism that they're not full-time teachers any more, yet they are passing on advice to those who are.

This is an interesting dilemma: to enable others to benefit from knowledge and experience requires such people to spend time communicating it to them, yet this often results in time away from the classroom, which can then affect the authenticity the speaker is perceived to have. I certainly came across this during my own training, when lecturers who had not been teaching in school for many years shared ideas of best practice with us. There were those whose response was along the lines of 'It's all very well them telling us how to do it, but when was the last time they were in a classroom?'

Some examples of best practice strike a chord; we can see how they address something we need to do or achieve, and in a way that would be appropriate for us, so we accept them and run with them. Other ideas will seem less useful and far removed from the context of our school or setting. For example, two schools might both be experiencing a challenge with getting boys engaged with writing. One school may have achieved great success using the cultural context of certain computer games to excite the boys' interest, but in the other, this may not be appropriate as many of the children are from low-income families who cannot afford to furnish them with such entertainment. The best practice of one can be of little use to the other.

Best practice is often used when making comparisons between schools. In the UK, this has taken the form of regular discussions about what might be learned from classroom practice in other countries that are perceived to be very successful. The Department for Education's recent review of the national curriculum in England has been influenced by a comprehensive review of 'best practice' in different subjects from across the world.[1] It is always interesting to make comparisons, especially when they are as diverse as those made between different countries, but there are also a number of problems with taking the data at face value.

Finland is often held up in the UK as an example of best practice due to the high levels achieved in international PISA league tables.[2] I have recently spent some time in a number of schools in Finland and, whilst I saw some excellent teaching, in many ways it was not significantly different to teaching in the UK. Finland's educational success is down to a whole range of factors of which the actual teaching practice is only a part. All Finnish teachers are required to complete their studies to master's level and places on these courses are highly competitive. The outcome of this is not just highly qualified teachers, but also a general perception that teachers are highly qualified and driven people, so teaching is highly valued in the public consciousness. As will be explored in Chapter 12, expectations can make all the difference, and these high expectations are coupled with an emphasis in Finnish culture on the importance of high achievement in school. This goes beyond merely practice examples; if we really want to closely replicate the perceived

---

1 Department for Education, *Review of the National Curriculum in England: What Can We Learn from the English, Mathematics and Science Curricula of High-Performing Jurisdictions?* Ref: DFE-RR178 (2011). Available at: www.education.gov.uk/publications/ standard/publicationDetail/Page1/DFE-RR178.

2 See, for example, OECD, *PISA 2009 Results: What Students Know and Can Do*. Available at: www.oecd.org/edu/pisa/2009.

Finnish success then we must also consider replicating these aspects of their culture.

Whilst these characteristics of education and culture in Finland are probably quite desirable to most British teachers, there are other aspects of Finnish society that are more problematic. For example, due to a range of historical factors Finland is much more culturally, economically and racially similar than the UK. This cultural homogeneity potentially contributes to their educational success, but it would be hard to make a case for improving British schools by making our country less ethnically and culturally diverse. Quite apart from what would be involved in implementing this suggestion being morally highly questionable, cultural diversity is also one of our biggest strengths as a nation.

So, when looking at international comparisons, best practice is only part of the story; culture and background are equally important in the success (or failure) of national education systems. This complexity is true to some degree in all scenarios of attempting to learn from best practice; whether it is the class next door or the school next door there will always be different cultural and situational factors. Bearing this in mind, some best practice can be shared more generally. Some approaches simply lend themselves to this more; others can be generalised due to the skills of gifted communicators who can adapt them for schools in different contexts.

We then move into a grey area between examples of best practice and theories of best practice. It is worth considering in some detail the differences between theory and practice in order to evaluate them clearly.

Best practice can be characterised as a collection of examples, of things that have worked in a classroom setting and are perceived to be effective enough to be passed on. Theory means taking this several steps further, and attempting not just to describe but to explain how or why something works or does not work. To return to Martin's knowledge funnel concept, best practice taken on its own can exist in the area of mystery. That is not to say best practice cannot be proven to produce results; within the context in which it takes place, it can be evaluated rigorously and shown to have had a significant effect, good or bad. What a best practice example, on its own, does not do is to break things down in such a way that shows *why* it worked; not the outcomes but the fundamental processes that enabled this to happen.

Approaches and concepts used as part of a best practice example are often eventually broken down into something that is more general. When a strategy is so successful as to be shared, people usually want to try to figure out why. It also helps to break the practice down into the key themes as this allows it to be formulated into a general rule that others can use. In the example mentioned above, of using computer games to encourage boys' writing, this could be generalised from one specific game to the use of games in general. It could also be taken further to examine why using computer games works, and perhaps be reframed using other contexts from a child's home culture to encourage engagement with writing. Another angle might be the fact that the computer game used had been recently released, so we might conclude that the defining factor for success was the use of very up-to-date cultural references. At this point, we move beyond a simple example of success in the world of mystery and towards Martin's concept of a heuristic – a rule or theory that can be understood and applied. From then on, it doesn't have to be executed in the specific format of the original example, but instead can be adapted in ways that leverage the underlying strengths of that example but in different contexts and in ways that can potentially make a difference to a much wider group of people.

In reality, this is happening all the time, whether through listening to speakers, reading about successful practitioners or seeing them acted out during classroom observations. We all look for patterns and heuristics, ways to adapt and fit the examples we see to the contexts we experience. However, it is worth questioning whether we are just taking an example and replicating it without considering how its underlying principles apply to us or whether we are being genuinely resourceful in our own practice.

Sometimes theories about teaching and learning emerge from the best practice that is happening in the classroom. This can take the shape of an individual's best practice being considered and communicated widely, leading to it being analysed on broader terms. A theory is, after all, simply a concept about how something works, and despite the grand terms in which they are valorised, can come from nothing more complicated than thinking something through. Traditionally, this has been in the form of someone coming up with an idea and then testing it to try to prove or disprove whether it works. The extent to which particular theories have been tested always varies, so this is something to consider before we decide what value to give them. For example, one of the most regularly cited theories by educators, Piaget's work on cognitive development, is often criticised as it was developed with only one child as its subject.

Educational theories often come from research in other fields, such as psychology – naturally, the study of how people think and behave has much relevance for teachers. This has given us such theories as Maslow's hierarchy of needs[3] and Daniel Willingham's models of how memory and thinking work.[4] Recently, interest has also been shown in applying theories and insights from areas such as neuroscience to education, with neuroscientist Paul Howard Jones exploring the new emerging field of 'neuroeducational research'.[5]

---

3 A. H. Maslow, A Theory of Human Motivation, *Psychological Review* 50(4) (1943): 370–396.

4 D. T. Willingham, *Why Don't Students Like School: A Cognitive Scientist Answers Questions About How the Mind Works and What It Means for the Classroom* (San Francisco, CA: Jossey Bass, 2009).

5 Howard Jones, *Introducing Neuroeducational Research*.

Despite coining the term for a new field, Howard Jones makes a vital point: to see his work as an attempt to simply translate the insights of neuroscience into how the brain works, and then apply them to education, is far from the point. In his book, he describes this as a dangerous approach for a number of reasons. The most important of these is that whilst neuroscience and education are areas of research with the aim of better understanding the world, they are coming at this from very different underpinnings of how that world works: neuroscience is concerned with the physical workings of the brain, whereas education is concerned with the mind.

The brain is a physical entity which works in particular ways that, whilst complex, can be proven or disproven. Things occur in the brain and these can be quantified and tested using scientific methods. The mind, on the other hand, is more slippery. The very idea of the mind is a human construct; it is reliant on the assumption that how we think and learn is influenced by, but different from, the chemical and physical processes in the brain. It is unthinkable that we could administer an injection of chemicals that would create the changes needed in the brain for a person to learn a skill such as how to ride a bike or a set of knowledge such as the storylines of the complete works of Shakespeare. These things require experiences and interactions. Granted, these may cause physical changes in the brain, but until we can shortcut these experiences and enact these changes more directly, it is more helpful to consider the effects they have on the mind and the way they shape the way we think.

Seeking to understand the brain and the mind are therefore very different: one is a 'hard' scientific study of physical processes, the other a 'soft' exploration of human constructs which have no tangible, physical existence. Both of these stances are based on different conceptions of the nature of reality. In science, when dealing with the physical world, it is necessary to adopt a position of there being facts and truths as things that can be seen and proved. In education, when exploring the mind, the concept of truth is more problematic – there may be a different version of truth for each person depending on their interpretation, or even many different versions within a single person's thinking depending on the particular situation.

Howard Jones makes the very valid point that it is hugely problematic to expect neuroscience and education, two fields with such different underlying approaches, to be able to share insights in a straightforward way. It might be tempting to say that all teachers should learn some neuroscience to help them better understand the effect they are having on their students' brains, but the reality is that although learning about this field may be hugely interesting, it is unlikely to give teachers much to go on when they are in the classroom. Howard Jones is seeking to bring together educators and neuroscientists in a productive dialogue where they can discuss their work, discover any regions of overlap and conduct more research into how these areas of understanding can further inform both fields. This is more complicated than simply learning a bit about neuroscience, but it is much more likely to yield useful results that have the potential to impact on learning.

This leads us to the common problem that many teachers have with theory. There is a sense that educational theory is often lacking in relevance in the complex and messy world of real classrooms. The fact that theory is usually broken down into the key concepts that can be applied across various settings can strip it of its context and make it appear that it has been constructed for a perfect world where other factors are not a problem – something that is far from the case in real schools. This is exacerbated by the fact that the theory may have emerged from another discipline (e.g. psychology), and whilst many teachers are searching for answers as to how processes in the mind, such as learning, take place, they do not necessarily share the underlying positions and assumptions of a psychologist.

This is quite apart from the fact that theories about learning, even those which have been rigorously tested and proven, often seem counterintuitive to what teachers see in the classroom every day. A great example of this is Alfie Kohn's work on rewards which, in a nutshell, suggests that not only do rewards not work but that they are actually harmful.[6] This is a difficult notion to take seriously as a primary school teacher, for example, who sees children behaving and performing academically for rewards on a daily basis. Taking on board these viewpoints requires considerable reflection, not to mention resolving the conflict that you may have spent an entire career wrongly giving children rewards. Much as the sharing of best practice can be open to challenges based on the transferability of their applicability and authenticity, those sharing education theory with teachers can easily be met with the response that the ideas might be 'all right in theory, but that's not what happens in my classroom'.

Head teacher Neil Hopkin asserts the need to replace the quest for 'best practice' with the search for 'next practice'.[7] I have always thought that aiming for today's best practice resulted in achieving the best of yesterday. By the time best practice has been devised, tested, assessed and shared with the teaching community, then it is already old news and things have moved on. By focusing on next practice, we keep things moving forward – constantly checking that what we are doing is the best solution for today rather than a reuse of what was best in the past.

This could take the form of a totally new approach devised from scratch, but more likely it is the case of looking at the best practice that is served up to you and asking the question, what next? This leads to adapting and developing best practice rather than just implementing it; a process which is more likely to result in careful consideration of all the contextual

---

6 A. Kohn, *Punished by Rewards: The Trouble with Gold Stars, Incentive Plans, A's, Praise, and Other Bribes.* (New York: Houghton Mifflin, 1999).

7 N. Hopkin, Energising Education, *Neil Hopkin's Blog* (6 December 2010). Available at: neilhopkin.wordpress.com/2010/12/06/energising-education/. See also R. Deakin Crick, H. Jelfs, S. Huang and Q. Wang, *Learning Futures Evaluation Final Report* (2011). Available at: learningemergence.net/technical-reports-2/learning-futures-evaluation-2011/.

differences between the school or class in which you are trying to implement it and therefore avoiding the problems discussed above. By aiming to invent the future rather than rehash the past, we will be creating the current best practice.

Of course, it is more complicated than this suggests. We will never reach our goal and stop, secure in the knowledge that we have found the best practice for us and our setting. Next practice is not about the goal, it is about the journey. A commitment to next practice is a commitment to continually develop what you are doing in the context in which it is situated. In most cases, this is going to require learning from others and assessing the current best practice, but fundamentally this is not about emulation – it is about a research-based approach to constant evaluation and development.

Next practice is a commitment to a process not an end product. In moving from best practice to next practice, we acknowledge that the best solutions come from development, not imposition. Perhaps a process of development that never stops should be our real goal. This approach would certainly be more challenging than implementing examples as is, but it would avoid many of the problems inherent in doing so. However, it would not address how to deal with the beneficial applications of more abstract theory.

I would argue that thinking about and using theory distinguishes teachers as professionals rather than just technicians. If teachers were technicians, then their role would be to apply the best practice set out to them as effectively and efficiently as possible without deviating too much from it. Clearly this is not what teachers do, and instead the role involves adapting, improving and creating their own practice in order to get the best outcomes from their students. To simply apply a theory you do not necessarily have to understand it; but to undertake the kind of constantly adapting and creative thinking required to fit teaching to the complex and varied requirements of young people demands a great deal of understanding. If an approach does not work as well as it could, then teachers need to be able to do more than just try plan B or plan C; they need to be able to understand why one strategy worked better than another and adapt what happens in their classrooms accordingly.

These decisions are based on understanding, and understanding teaching and learning is based on more than just a series of examples about how to do things. Real understanding means appreciating not just *what* is happening but *why* it is happening. Theories don't tell teachers what to do, but instead provide a structure in which to think about what they do.

However, it is more complicated than simply building up a stockpile of theoretical knowledge about teaching and then applying it in the classroom. Even newly qualified teachers with a dose of theory about learning bring with them considerable experience, notably their experience of learning during their own education. We do not come to theory cold; we use our own experience to understand it. It is not a case of learning then implementing, but more a more complicated cycling between specific examples from memory or experience and new abstract understanding.

This works the other way as well: experience can also shape the way we think about a theory. Whilst the initial thinking around planning some learning might be influenced by a theoretical understanding, when this gets put to the test in the classroom our knowledge will develop. So, your theoretical framework influences your practice, but your experience in the classroom also continues to shape your framework; the two are not separate.

The Brazilian educator and theorist Paulo Freire used a different term to describe this unity between theory and practice: *praxis*.[8] This can be summed up as 'informed action' – the process of taking practical action

---

8 P. Freire, *Pedagogy of the Oppressed* (New York: Penguin, 1970).

whilst acting within a theoretical framework. In praxis, theory and practice are as one. As with any theory, and the concept of praxis is just a theory, it is important to understand where it is coming from to better understand its subtleties, its intended purpose and the assumptions on which it is based.

Freire's childhood was marked by the poverty of the Great Depression of the 1930s, and his later work was concerned with the potential of education to empower the poor and the oppressed in society, particularly in South America. He saw education as inherently political, a force to empower individuals by giving them the tools to re-imagine themselves and take control of their lives. His theories were born out of a view of education not as something to prepare individuals to live in the world, but to equip them to change it, and, particularly for those traditionally marginalised by the world, to make the changes needed to achieve social justice. Freire's revolutionary politics did not make a distinction between thinking differently and making a concrete change in the world. To create this kind of social change requires action, but it also requires complex thinking; the two cannot be separated.

In praxis, abstract theorising is only useful as long as it informs concrete action; likewise, action must be informed by deep thinking. Only by the combining the two did Freire believe that 'the oppressed' could find their own 'new' way to intellectual and social freedom, rather than simply repeating the mistakes of their 'oppressors' and becoming the same as them. They had to think differently and live out this thinking in direct action.

For teachers who believe that education is about maintaining the status quo and preparing young people to fit into their place in society, it might be difficult to assimilate Freire's theory with its revolutionary roots. If schools exist to replicate the status quo, then perhaps praxis is not what we need at all. But then neither would we need thinking teachers – we would be quite well equipped with people who can carry out the teaching they are told to deliver.

In the last few decades, a tradition of 'reflective practice' has built up in education, emphasising the need for practitioners to evaluate their practice in order to learn from it. This has some similarities with the concept of praxis, particularly as it links the action of practice with the thinking of reflection. Donald Schon's concepts of 'reflection on action' and 'reflection in action'[9] have been assimilated by many teacher-training institutions, and most teachers are encouraged to continue learning from their practice by reflecting on it afterwards and considering how they could move forward, whether this takes the form of annotating lesson plans, a reflective diary or just thinking about it. Reflection in action is given less attention, but it also has links to praxis in that it involves making use of previous experience and professional expertise to make changes that will improve practice. This is the idea of 'thinking on your feet' that is often so necessary in the classroom.

The key difference is that reflection is quite insular; it is about you, your experience and your feelings about your practice. Being reflective is largely about shifting your practice from the baseline to something better, but using your own practice as the main source of information and insight. Praxis is not a case of 'doing' and then 'reflecting' on it later; rather, it means making sure every action has an informed basis and every valuable thought is put into action. A teacher involved in bringing theory into practice could consider their actions when planning, and then again when reflecting or evaluating on it. A teacher immersed in praxis would bring their theoretical thoughts to bear on every decision as they make it, adapting their actions in a classroom to ensure they continue to encourage learning.

9 D. Schon, *Educating the Reflective Practitioner* (Chichester: John Wiley & Sons, 1987).

Whilst reflection is a powerful tool for improving your practice, praxis is something quite different; it can lead to the 'next practice' that moves teaching and learning forward by taking onboard influences from others. This aim chimes with Freire's objective that education should be about allowing people to shape the world rather than just survive in it.

Teaching is a complex business of both practical action and intellectual consideration. Often, we define these two facets as distinct when, in reality, they are a continuum and we usually exist at some point in the middle. Best practice examples can shine an interesting light on what we do, but it is important to remember that we are always considering them based on the heuristics built from our own experience and theoretical understanding. Likewise, theory can develop our understanding of what is happening in our classrooms, but it is ultimately only of use in influencing our practice and thereby the learning of the young people we work with. So often we think about either theory or practice when we would do well to heed Freire's call to 'informed action'.

Chapter 7

Regulation: lessons from finance

Shifting goalposts, lack of certainty, changes in public opinion; these are just a few factors currently affecting the teaching profession. Our society is also changing in many ways, with new technologies affecting the way we interact, migration changing the cultural make-up of our communities and culture changing the way young people respond to schools and learning. It often seems like nothing is changing as much as government education policy, and this, above all, has a significant impact on the expectations set for teachers and their students.

At present we are experiencing a strong swing in education policy in the UK. Under the Labour government of 1997–2010, many education policies had a distinctly holistic flavour. Social and Emotional Aspects of Learning (SEAL) encouraged schools to teach students about personal attributes and relationship skills. Every Child Matters encouraged joined-up working with other social services. Even the name of the government department with overall responsibility for schools changed from the Department of Education to the Department for Children, Schools and Families (DCSF), reflecting this holistic approach to the lives of children.

In 2009, two reports were published into the future of primary education, one commissioned by the government and one truly independent.[1] Both recommended a significant shift towards cross-curricular learning that would follow themes rather than traditional subjects, thereby

---

1 See J. Rose, *Independent Review of the Primary Curriculum: Final Report* [Rose Review] (Nottingham: DCSF, 2009). Available at: www.education.gov.uk/publications/ eOrderingDownload/Primary_curriculum_Report.pdf; and R. Alexander (ed.), *Children, their World, their Education: Final Report and Recommendations of the Cambridge Primary Review* (London: Routledge, 2009).

enabling links to be made across the learning happening in schools. However, it only took one year and a change in government to begin another significant shift. The DCSF became the Department for Education, both reports were denounced and a new curriculum was drafted using the traditional subject boundaries, with the Secretary of State for Education emphasising that it was his belief that the central function of schools was academic study.

For teachers and school leaders, all these changes have led to a pressure to try to stay ahead of the curve. In the case of the recent curriculum changes, many primary schools had decided to implement the changes to the curriculum outlined by the Rose Review. For example, new staff were recruited to lead the change in focus for ICT to become a core subject alongside literacy and numeracy. In this area the pendulum has truly swung, if not in the opposite direction then certainly in a different one: ICT is no longer even a subject in the new curriculum as set out by the present coalition government. This is to say nothing of continuing changes to GCSE and A level exams in the secondary sector, and the constantly shifting landscape of funding for Early Years education.

In just a few years, the pendulum of policy has swung from one extreme to the other – and schooling is just one example of how political changes have led to huge shifts and uncertainty for certain professions. It might seem an unusual, and even an unwelcome, comparison but there are some interesting parallels to be drawn between education and the banking industry. Whilst children and money are clearly very different, examining how other industries deal with problems can allow us to step back and consider what interesting solutions might emerge for teaching and learning.

Since the financial crisis of 2008, the finance sector has undergone much change. The recession in the UK and other parts of the world has caused a significant shift in the way the industry is dealt with by government, a shift that in some ways mirrors the swing in curriculum policy experienced by schools. Many would argue that the changes to the banking sector have been brought about due to the irresponsible activities of many of those in the industry, whereas the changes in education have been influenced by the shifting ideologies of those in power. That may be, but the end result is a situation sufficiently similar to hold some interesting comparisons.

In the wake of the financial crisis, one of the hottest topics in banking and finance has been regulation. Since the crisis took hold, and a number of UK banks received sizeable bailouts from the government, the controls on them have been significantly tightened. In an attempt to prevent what the media has regularly characterised as reckless practices, measures have been put in place affecting the size of trades banks can make and the amount of money they must have in their accounts to 'back up' transactions. If these rules are broken sanctions are imposed, so banks can now be fined for taking actions that were once common practice.

Entire conferences have been based around exploring how to deal with these increased controls. A senior banker at the 2013 SWIFT Business Forum which I attended claimed (and was not contested) that most financiers spend around fifty per cent of their time managing the compliance measures set by governments in order to avoid the complex systems of sanctions that are imposed should they transgress these rules.

Compare this situation to the 'regulation' faced by schools that have to undergo inspection. In England this is Ofsted, whose visits are often spoken of with trepidation and whose opinion is considered before many school management decisions are taken. Ofsted consider a number of aspects before making a judgement on how effective a school is in specific areas and overall. The Ofsted framework changes with some regularity, as does the emphasis in terms of which areas are deemed to be of most importance. Previously there have been frameworks that placed a great emphasis on the leadership and management of a school, whilst the 2013 framework places more weight on the quality of teaching. For our comparison with the banking sector, there are two discrete areas to consider: exams and assessment results, and the methods schools use to achieve those results.

The outcomes of a school could be defined as being the results that young people get in national tests or exams, although few would argue that these are the *only* outcomes that matter. Other outcomes are often harder to measure: the confidence of young people and their capacity to learn, sporting achievement and the involvement of students in their communities. Even a small selection of Ofsted reports shows that inspectors use many of these 'outputs' to measure the effectiveness of a school.

However, Ofsted do not only measure outputs – they also measure processes. One current key focus of inspections is the 'quality of teaching', a measure that involves inspectors watching teachers teach and making a judgement on the quality of the processes of teaching and learning that are taking place. If some outcomes are hard to measure objectively, measuring the quality of the process of teaching is no less so. Hence, we have endless debates and second-guessing about what Ofsted are looking for, and the widely acknowledged game whereby teachers presented with the prospect of an inspector at the back of the room change the way they teach in order to fit with the way they think someone else thinks they should be doing things. That is quite a chain of thinking.

The regulation of the business world brings a different perspective to the education system. Some would argue that there is a case for an educational 'free market', where no regulation gives parents a free choice about where to send their children; instead, the market forces of supply and demand allow the best educational provision to rise to the top. Amongst the many problems with this is idea is that, unlike many aspects of the economy, children only get one chance at an education, so most of us would conclude that some level of regulation is needed lest those disadvantaged in terms of income, geographic location or even just how informed their parents are, are left without an adequate education. The free market could easily run away with itself, taking with it the chances of underprivileged children.

The case for regulation is therefore quite strong, but the question lies in what type of regulation and how closely the education system should be regulated. To many teachers, the very idea of 'government regulation' implies strict checks, rules and measures. Teachers often complain about the disproportionate level of influence inspection has on the way they go about their jobs. Over-regulation can lead to distortions in the very thing it is designed to be checking.

According to the ex-chairman of Royal Dutch Shell, Sir Mark Moody Stuart, regulation is usually concerned with controlling processes rather than controlling outcomes. To illustrate this, he cites the legislation around catalytic convertors in vehicles. This regulation is successful in that it meets the goals it is designed to address, but Moody Stuart argues that it has also resulted in an almost total lack of innovation in this field for decades. With such tight controls on how catalytic convertors are made, there is little that can be done to achieve the desired goal more efficiently or at a lower cost by using different materials or developing alternative ways of reaching that goal.

If catalytic convertor legislation was based on outcomes instead of processes, the result that it is designed to produce would be the same, but manufacturers would be free to innovate with different systems and materials to achieve that end result. The outcome would still be regulated, so it could not get worse, but innovation might result in achieving this in ways that were cheaper for the consumer or more elegant. Moody Stuart call this 'smart regulation' – regulation that is concentrated on the things that really matter, the outcomes, and that allows enough space for the ways in which these goals are achieved to be developed.

This way of looking at the discrete regulation of process and outcome casts an interesting light on some of the regulation in English schools. Where do we currently regulate for outcomes and leave the process free for innovation? Where are we regulating the actual process? Examples of both can be found. Schools are often judged and regulated by their outcomes; whether this is SAT scores or GCSE and A level results, such scores are perceived to be a measure of a school's success and will inform where schools are placed on league tables, thereby affecting the decisions parents make when choosing schools and the likelihood of a school being inspected.

However, when an inspection occurs, even a school that is seen to be reaching or exceeding the required outcomes will have their processes placed under scrutiny in the form of lesson observations. This is when we move into an area where processes themselves are potentially being regulated, particularly if a certain style of teaching is expected. Examples of good practice often convince teachers to adopt a particular teaching style, as do published inspection reports praising certain styles of teaching and anecdotes from colleagues who have been judged to be outstanding. As mentioned above, many teachers feel the need to create a performance under inspection conditions. Under normal circumstances they may be innovative practitioners but revert to the methods they think are expected when it comes to an inspection.

Moreover, the regulation of process goes even deeper. Many teachers choose to share their good practice in an attempt to learn from each other, whether informally through networks of friends, more formally by presenting at teacher conferences or by publishing their resources, plans or reflections online. Whilst inspection creates a well-recognised pressure to conform to a certain style, the sharing of good practice also creates an arena in which we look at examples of teaching and judge them by the merit of their processes rather than their outcomes. How often have you chosen to implement an idea or a type of lesson based on the reported results it has received, rather than because you thought it seemed new and interesting? Most of us have done this many times, thereby helping to support an informal regulation of teaching processes rather than outcomes.

Under Moody Stuart's model, all regulation of process potentially constrains innovation in the classroom as it creates the perception that there is a particular way that things should be done in order to achieve certain outcomes. If we were instead to implement a model of 'smart regulation' in schools, we would simply put in place required standards for outcomes and measure only those. This would leave teachers free to innovate with their methods and potentially allow them to find more efficient ways of reaching those outcomes, or more effective ways to achieve even better outcomes.

Of course, it isn't as simple as that; it is all very well to decide to regulate purely for outcomes, but we might need to reach a more consistent agreement on the desirable outcomes of education. One-time summative testing is a fairly straightforward result by which to set targets, but teachers, parents and young people are far from being in agreement that this is an outcome they desire. Some would argue that what matters are longer term outcomes such as success in the job market, others that well-being and happiness indexes should be the aim. An argument for 'smart regulation' in education is not necessarily an argument for placing existing exams at the centre; instead, it opens up a debate about what outcomes we should be aiming for.

With the current marketisation of some aspects of British education, there is value in looking at some of these models from the world of economics to see what insights we might gain into where we are in education and where we might be headed. The current system regulates both outcomes (in the form of results and targets) and process (in the form of Ofsted inspections, although that is, of course, not their only focus). Would a move to Moody Stuart's smart regulation allow space for innovation and improvement whilst giving us the accountability and checks needed to ensure young people are getting the education to which they are entitled?

In some ways the business framework is about as far as you could get from the values and norms of teaching, but that is entirely why it is so powerful to consider what light it might throw on education.

Chapter 8

Minimum viable lessons

There can be few situations more stressful than starting up a new enterprise from scratch. It is a risky business – often people starting out on this process have given up a secure or salaried job to develop an idea. Most likely it will be solely up to the individual(s) in question to take the necessary action that will turn it from an idea without substance into a business that can support them. This creates an interesting set of conditions under which people think quite differently about what they are doing when compared with a job like teaching, which, whilst often being challenging and stressful, is usually financially secure. Also, by working as part of a large school team you have colleagues who can lean on each other to deliver results.

Start-up entrepreneurs have to believe in their idea strongly, especially if they have given up financial security or lots of their free time to make it into a reality. Sometimes these are ideas that an individual may have been churning over slowly for years; or they might be based on a sense that they can solve a certain problem or situation in a different or better way; or that they have come up with an idea that has never been tried before. Many people harbour their dreams for a long time before taking the plunge and trying to make them a reality; many never do. Often, the final trigger for turning ideas into action can come years after the original idea. It may have grown from an initial spark and been developed through late-night conversations and musings to the point where so much time has been invested in it, or it has been tried and tested by so much criticism from friends, that it just has to be tried. It may be that an idea that had initially seemed unachievable becomes possible due to changes in technology or from acquiring new learning and skills.

Often these ideas grow out of a passion, such as the children's app and website Night Zookeeper. Over the last few years, the small team of friends involved in this enterprise have seemingly come out of nowhere, winning competition after competition for start-up businesses and releasing two apps in the last six months to critical acclaim. However, their story goes back well before the mobile app was a common phenomenon. Their journey began in the mid-2000s, with the passion of two university friends for bringing storytelling and creative visual arts to children. They wrote a children's story, did some workshops with schools and then moved on to other things. However, the idea continued to grow and be discussed for years until they realised that it had the potential to become something big, eventually prompting the pair to leave jobs in Qatar and Washington and return, jobless, to the UK to make a go of it.

Some ideas mature more quickly – in a moment of inspiration, someone spots a problem or a solution and decides to run with it and take the risk. However, to really get a business idea moving and developing into something with a future takes time. Some people invest this time in their evenings and weekends, often committing much of the time outside their day job to making it into a reality. Others take the plunge and quit their jobs, giving up financial security and often investing savings or borrowing money from friends and family.

To invest your precious savings in a business requires huge self-belief, so it also creates considerable pressure. There is only so long you can tolerate giving up all your free time to your venture, only so long you can survive without a regular income, and only so much of friends' and families' generosity you can sink into a business before you have to show a return, or at least some kind of result that will attract the attention of others to believe in the idea as much as you do, and support it.

This can create difficulties. To have even begun to realise an idea takes tremendous belief in its potential to succeed. You would not take on such an enterprise unless you thought the idea had the potential to be significant. Equally, taking it on with any degree of seriousness involves imposing a huge set of constraints on the business in terms of money and time, thereby creating a considerable pressure to deliver as quickly as possible. It is the temptation to take it as far as it can go versus the pressure to deliver it yesterday. Enter the concept of a 'minimum viable product'.

The minimum viable product is the *least* you need for success; the simplest implementation of an idea that is capable of supporting itself. In the case of a business idea, this would be the simplest version of a product or service that people would be willing to pay for at a price and in sufficient numbers to make enough money to sustain the company. To create such a product inevitably involves some compromises, particularly when the idea has been brewing for some time and has been conceived as something that could be really big. However, whilst it can seem like a concession to boil something down to its very simplest form, it can also bring an elegance which has significant benefits.

One of the first people to really make me think about this idea was Henry Playfoot of Stealth Education who produced a minimum viable product in the form of his iPhone app, ABC Spy. It is a great example of the power of simplicity, both as a product and as a learning activity. The app presents children with the opportunity to make their own ABC book, but instead of the book being based around the standard clip art of animals or toys starting with each letter, it encourages them to find and photograph objects that start with each letter using the phone's in-built camera.

It is a simple concept, yet very elegant. Context and connections are so important for young children, and enabling them to use objects from their own lives to support learning the alphabet is powerful. The app makes children think about how and where to find the objects, rather than just serving it up to them in an engaging way. For some letters this will be quite straightforward, but for others it takes some effort to find an object in their day-to-day lives. As well as thinking of the object, they will also have to find them, increasing the amount of time and thought that goes into the activity. As an app that is meant to be entertaining, this adds to the challenge, but the longer children engage with the thought processes, the more likely they are to cement the letters they are looking for in their head. This simple construct creates a number of benefits.

The app also solves another problem: young children really love taking photos but often lack direction and focus. Give a camera to a 5-year-old and they often take a large number of pictures without much purpose. ABC Spy gives them a purpose for their photographs, not in the form of a torrent of specific instructions but with an undemanding structure: photograph things that start with these letters. It is easy to follow but also open-ended and creative enough to create a long stream of activity without further direction. Crucially, it also means that after an initial introduction from an adult, children can continue to use the app and learn their letters independently.

On the face of it, the situation of a start-up entrepreneur – with high levels of risk and the pressures of time and money to create an end-product – seems quite different from that of a teacher. However, there is much to be taken away from this way of thinking that could shape a different way of planning and designing lessons and learning experiences.

To begin with, the pressure on time is an all too familiar problem for most teachers. With the limited time often available, it could help to think about what a 'minimum viable lesson' might look like. By its very nature, planning never produces a full representation of a lesson, rather it is a basic structure and the gaps are filled in as it takes place. Sometimes this will be supplemented by the knowledge of the teacher, and at other times it is extended by the learners as they undertake an activity and flesh out the instructions in the way they interact, discuss, create or apply the lesson plan.

Whilst saving time and paperwork might be a desirable side-effect, a minimum viable lesson is about more than simply cutting down on detail or saving time. It is about getting the most out of the least; finding the most elegant solution to a learning problem. This requires a shift in thinking – from creating lessons as sets of instructions to be followed to structures that frame the learning.

Learning and creativity consultant Ewan McIntosh has coined the phrase 'fewer instructions, better structures' when working with teachers to explore how they can plan for open-ended projects with young people.[1] In his work with games designers, McIntosh noticed that the games that tend to turn players off are the ones with too many instructions. The games that get the best engagement, and hence the best reviews, are the ones that are structured in such a way that players intuitively know where they are and what they are doing and can concentrate on the task in hand independently. In the computer games world, if you turn players off by having too many instructions, you lose them and they find another game to play.

In school, most young people do not have the luxury of walking away, although their attention certainly does. One of the reasons we can end up with too many instructions in lessons is the constant quest for novelty, not just in what we teach but the way that we teach it. In fact, with curricula and exam specifications to meet, there is often very little novelty in what we teach, so the temptation is to inject that into how we do it. Creative teachers are on a constant search to find novel ways of delivering that same lesson. The problem is that the more novel the lesson structure, the more working memory the learners have to devote to following the instructions, and therefore less is available for whatever learning is meant to be the main focus of the lesson. We can all remember occasions when lessons have been interrupted too many times by

---

1 E. McIntosh, Fewer Instructions, Better Structures, *Ewan McIntosh's edu.blogs* (18 May 2011). Available at: edu.blogs.com/edublogs/2011/05/fewer-instructions-better-structures.html.

students asking for clarification about what they should be doing, or when we have noticed some time into the activity that the group isn't actually doing what they were meant to be doing and we have had to stop and repeat the instructions.

The solution to this is to make lessons less novel; rather than having a new set of instructions every lesson, have some set structures that you follow, discuss them explicitly, and let the learners you teach become very familiar with them. Clearly, not all lesson ideas will work in this way – some are too specific or not flexible enough to be reused over and over with different content. If you want to design minimal viable lessons, then it may be time to drop those ideas. This might mean letting go of some lessons that you have brought out once a year for some time. It might also mean not jumping on that off-the-wall idea for a lesson inspired by something you came across at the weekend. However, what it will do is to make you focus on the best of what you do, and focus on refining that rather than constantly looking for something new.

Kagan Cooperative Learning uses structures in a very explicit way to organise learning activities.[2] Although it is particularly designed to organise groups working and learning together, Dr Spencer Kagan also suggests basing lessons around a set of well-known structures to cut down on the number of instructions and focus the learners on the learning rather than the doing of a lesson. The Kagan system is based around groups of four students, with very specific rules for interaction. For example, the most straightforward structure, the Round Robin involves moving clockwise around the group with each person having a turn to give their answer or opinion. More complex structures involve cards of questions which are moved around the group in a specific way to ensure all learners have a chance to both ask and answer a question and respond to someone else's answer. There is a certain amount of explicit teaching involved in getting these structures across, and in the Kagan system it

---

2 S. Kagan, *Kagan Cooperative Learning* (San Clemente, CA: Kagan Publishing, 2001).

is recommended that this happens in a light-hearted and undemanding context, so that the learners can concentrate fully on the instructions. Crucially, though, once these have been learned the structure can be used again and again. For example, in the activities described above, the questions used can be changed to focus on almost any content, and whilst certain structures may be more appropriate for certain types of content, the idea is that they are flexible and portable. Tell a class trained in Kagan structures to do a Fan and Pick activity based on the five questions you give them, and they will all know what to do to get straight into the task. More importantly, they can concentrate on the questions and their responses to them rather than any new instructions.

Many teachers spend a huge amount of time working to engage children by situating their lessons within contexts that are likely to be meaningful to them. For the teacher of younger children, this might mean using a popular television programme or computer game character to engage children in learning to write. Finding out which characters engage the children is only the start though; for the activity to be meaningful, the teacher will have to find out as much as they can about the character in order to set up the task. Then the activity itself must be designed to take all of this into account. This is not only the case when teaching younger children. Most of us have tried to engage our learners by closely designing the learning around a context we think will be engaging and culturally relevant to them, such as current news stories, sports teams or books they are reading.

There is no guarantee that all of the learners in a class are going to be engaged by the same topic. In fact, contexts deeply rooted in young people's popular culture can often have as many adverse reactions as positive ones. It can therefore backfire, especially with teenagers; the more strongly positive one group feels about a particular context, the more likely another group will feel equally strongly about it from a negative perspective.

What matters is not the details of how a theme from popular culture can be made to fit with pre-defined curriculum areas but that the context of the learning is meaningful. That which is meaningful can often be unfamiliar. Rather than trying to bring familiarity to a learning context by drawing links in explicit detail, a minimum viable lesson might be built around a theme or an idea that will resonate with learners and allow them to bring their own reactions and contexts to it, whilst also providing them with content and learning that is new.

One approach to teaching and learning that uses a similar methodology is Design Thinking, which has been adapted from the design and creative industries. As with many educational approaches, different people have used this label for some quite different methods, but my thinking in this area has been specifically influenced by Ewan McIntosh (discussed above). Design Thinking is a structure for project-based learning based on a five-stage process: empathy, definition, ideation, prototyping and evaluation. In his powerful TEDx talk,[3] McIntosh describes how in the traditional process of lesson design, the teacher is the one who does the hard work of exploring an area with which to contextualise learning.

He argues that learners should be fully involved in this process. After being introduced to a topic, rather than the teacher defining the problems or objectives they need to solve, the learners should explore the subject and seek out those areas that pose problems which are worth solving. They then move through the structure to find ways to solve these problems and develop any that stand a chance of being successful.

An approach to learning based on structures such as this requires a different process for planning. The traditional approach would be for a teacher divergently exploring an area, converging on the areas they wish to use for their lessons and then planning to deliver these specific areas.

---

3 E. McIntosh, Ewan McIntosh #TEDxLondon: The Problem Finders, *Ewan McIntosh's edu. blogs.com* (18 September 2011). Available at: edu.blogs.com/edublogs/2011/09/ewan-mcintosh-tedxlondon-the-problem-finders.html.

Structured approaches for allowing learners choice in their direction can involve planning a subject area in terms of provocations, where a body of knowledge and understanding are explored with the potential for multiple directions to be taken. The more choice of direction, the more relevant the project can be as it allows learners to bring their own experiences, challenges and problems to bear on the context. Rather than planning for specific pathways, this is a case of planning for possibilities, for the directions learning might take in the chosen context. This is conceptually similar to the way many teachers of the youngest children plan, and requires an in depth understanding of the area being explored. Preparing for possibilities might leave fewer instructions on the lesson plan, and hence create a 'minimum viable lesson', but it takes significant divergent thinking on behalf of the teacher to be able to respond in a constructive way to the directions the learners take.

In one sense, such plans could be depicted as 'minimal' because there are less specific instructions for activities pre-planned by teachers and mandated. In another the planning stage is more complex as a rich and immersive context needs to be found, developed and resourced.

One key aim of a Design Thinking approach to learning is that by including learners in the initial process of exploring an area and defining the problems they want to solve, it allows for unknown outcomes which may possibly solve new problems. This is an area where these types of structure can excel. Lessons closely designed around a set of instructions will usually lead to a specific end-point – following directions gets you to a specific outcome, in a specific way, through a specific context. In contrast, a Design Thinking structure allows for unknowns by building in space for them to occur.

The temptation when planning lessons is to build and build, adding details and instructions to try to ensure that nothing falls through the gaps. What if, instead, we approached lesson planning by looking at what would be the least we need to plan to enable success, that is, the minimum viable lesson? Repeating and reusing lesson structures rather than always running after the next novelty can enable learners to understand where they are in the process and focus on the learning rather than yet another new set of instructions. The more detail you can remove from a plan, the more space you leave for learners to make their own connections to the learning, and try out their own ways of using and applying it in contexts that make sense for them. Those spaces need to be clearly planned and designed for, with support on hand to make sure the contexts chosen are fit for purpose. Remember that the learning conversations that happen around such decisions are also valuable in themselves.

As in the business examples explored in this chapter, minimum viable lessons could be a way to get things moving in the classroom, enabling teachers to adapt as necessary based on the responses and reactions of our students, in a context that engages them, but all the while keeping the focus on the learning. However, whenever you open up the learning happening in a classroom to more variety and choice, there is a risk that less learning actually happens. Good instructions allow teachers to keep a tight control on what happens in their classrooms; after all, they are responsible for making sure that learning occurs and the curriculum gets covered.

For the thinking teacher, structures and instructions are tools to be deployed when the time is right. The most important factor is considering why these strategies are being deployed and the effects on learning. Thinking through the value of these positions means they will be implemented only when it is appropriate to do so.

Chapter 9

Worse is better

The world of computing has some interesting lessons for those of us working with the ultimate software – young people's minds. Although computers might seem far removed from the way people work, some thinking that has grown out of this area provides an interesting perspective on the way we think about teaching and learning.

In 1995, programmer Mike Gancarz developed an entire philosophy based on the principles of best practice when working with Unix operating systems.[1] Invented in 1969, Unix is arguably the longest lived computer operating system – versions of it are still in use and evolving today, with variants running the majority of the servers that power the internet and most smartphones. In an area of great change, Unix has stood the test of time, although it has mutated far from its original roots.

In fact, it is this mutation that has enabled Unix's longevity; without the ability to mutate and adapt there is little chance that a system originally designed for a handful of mainframe computers the size of a room could run most of the one billion smartphones that now fit in people's pockets.[2] Herein lies the first lesson for education: things spread if they are originally designed to be adaptable and to be built on by others. When designing lessons or learning experiences, how often do we consider how they could be modified by the input of our end users? A lesson on its own is just that, a tightly controlled moment in time with a specified

---

1 M. Gancarz, *The Unix Philosophy* (Boston, MA: Butterworth-Heinemann, 1995).

2 K. Rushton, Number of Smartphones Tops One Billion, *The Telegraph* (17 October 2012). Available at: www.telegraph.co.uk/finance/9616011/Number-of-smartphones-tops-one-billion.html.

start and end point. A lesson designed to be a starting point that could be taken further by the learners is potentially far more powerful, but designing lessons like these requires a very different perspective from the start.

Twenty-six years after Unix's initial development, and before it had reached the level of use we see today, Gancarz encapsulated the key principles he saw being enacted by those using and developing this system. His principles provide an interesting insight into a values-based approach to development; whilst some of these are specific to the realm of IT, many provide some interesting perspectives on other fields, such as education. I will consider five of these below.

The first principle is the one most obviously transferable to learning: *small is beautiful*. It is a well-recognised fact that keeping things small and discrete makes them easier to deal with, so, in teaching, large topics are carved up into smaller areas. The smaller a concept is, the more straightforward it is to explain, to understand and therefore to teach successfully. It also makes it more clear-cut to assess. Small is beautiful is evident in a lot of teaching and learning design already, although it is always worth remembering as the temptation to over-explain and over-complicate is ever present. But beware: the smaller you go, the less contextualised an idea can become. The more you hone in on it, the more it may potentially be perceived as something to learn just for the sake of it with little reason why. It is therefore important to couple this with an approach that has regular spaces for fitting the small and beautiful parts back together again, to guard against them becoming just another point to tick off with little connection to the larger picture.

The key insight of Gancarz's small is beautiful assertion is particularly associated with its computer programming roots. He argues that the main strength of small programs is that they can combine with other small programs in 'unique and useful ways'.[3] Think of the many things you can do with Microsoft Word or similar software. These programs are flexible; however, once you hit their limitations you have to wait for Microsoft to add extra functionality to their huge product. If it was instead carved up into smaller programs that worked together in a modular way, then if you needed to add something new someone could write a small program and it could talk to the existing programs and make that happen. Small applications can combine in ways that might not have been imagined by their creators – you only have to look at the inventive use of Lego by young children to see this in action. Whilst Lego may be sold in specific kits with sets of instructions on how to make a particular spacecraft, more often than not these are adapted and deconstructed to make something completely new.

The smaller the blocks that learning can be broken down into, the more potential there is for combining them in 'unique and useful ways'. In some senses, this is the essence of true understanding. For example, take a process of mathematical calculation such as the widely maligned long division. (In the case of maths, small really is beautiful: the small chunks of learning make it ripe for elegant examples that are not muddied by too many surrounding details.) Long division is something that I struggled with throughout my study of mathematics. I learnt how to do it as a single monolithic process, working from A to B, but I never really understood how each step worked and why it mattered. The result was that even towards the end of my A level maths studies, I found I had to relearn the process when applying it to algebra. I could complete a problem successfully after a little revision, but I could never use any of the underlying concepts in other situations. Because I had never understood the small pieces of this process, I floundered if I met a problem that required applying the elements in a way that was different to the questions with which I was familiar. In this example, an understanding of all the different elements of long division would likely have helped me to

---

3 Gancarz, *The Unix Philososphy*, p. 4.

remember it better, but it would also have allowed me to take each of those pieces and apply them in other contexts. Small is not just beautiful; small learning is the essence of true understanding.

The second principle of the Unix philosophy concerns interactivity – another regular feature of debates about education. Gancarz's principles decree that programmers should *avoid captive user interfaces*. Years ago, software was designed to do only one thing at a time. If you instructed it to perform a task, in the majority of cases, you had to wait until it had finished processing that task before it could begin on the next task; it held you captive with a blinking cursor until it had finished. These days we are largely used to not being held up by our computers. Usually, if they are performing a big task, we can carry on with something else – at the very least we can go off to another application and check our emails while we wait for that CD to rip or that video to export.

Whilst we take this for granted, how often do we think about the interface learners have with our teaching and whether they are held captive by it? The way we work in schools has a lot of potential to hold learners captive. On a simple level, this could be the child who manages to complete the particular objective of a lesson before that lesson comes to an end. In the case of many task-based lessons this is usually quite obvious, and teachers are well used to considering extensions as part of the planning process. Hopefully such extensions are genuinely extending the learning rather than simply the time spent on it, allowing for next steps rather than more of the same.

To consider this more deeply, we need to move beyond simply thinking about the tasks themselves and concentrate on the actual learning. With many learning objectives, it is possible that a child could have achieved the objective and learned what they need to well before they actually finish the set task. A simple example might be learning a mathematical calculation process, where a class is provided with progressively more difficult calculations to complete. It is perfectly possible that they could have learnt all the important principles before completing all of the calculations. If they are expected to finish all of them regardless, then their attention is being held captive by the user interface of the classroom – and surely it would be better if it could be released to move on to the next step in the learning rather than the next step in a linear task.

Despite this, there is still a case for hard work, practice and perseverance. Sometimes working through a task from start to finish, whether or not you are learning from every aspect of it, can be beneficial. However, we should be considering whether the way we design lessons and experiences for our students has the potential to hold them captive.

The third principle of the Unix philosophy is the assertion that *silence is golden*. Despite the importance of talk for learning, there are doubtless many teachers and those who spend any time with children and young people, for whom this has an immediate and literal appeal! Appealing though it might be, in the Unix philosophy this is meant less literally and relates to designing software that gets on with performing its function rather than providing the user with large numbers of error messages when things do not go as expected or progress messages when they do. From the perspective of lots of computer users this might seem odd – surely it's a good thing to give the user lots of information about what is happening. However, to understand why this might not be so desirable, you only have to consider the number of times messages pop up on your computer to tell you about nearby wireless hotspots when you are trying to read something, the latest updates when you are trying to get something written or ask 'are you sure?' questions when you just want to turn the machine off and go home.

Teachers tend to be more focused in their feedback, but they do provide an awful lot of it. The notion of scaffolding – carefully supporting learners to reach the steps just beyond their grasp – can lead to a lot of jumping in, asking questions or providing reassurance. Just as the error message or extra information can become distracting from the task you are trying to complete on your computer, overzealous feedback can also distract from the thought processes that learners are trying to carve out for themselves. Over-scaffolding can actually be a distraction. Perhaps consider this during interactions in the classroom; take a mental step back and ask whether silence might be more golden than support in this instance.

In many ways, this chimes with maths teacher and curriculum designer Dan Meyer's concept of 'being less helpful'.[4] Meyer argues that all too often we provide learners with far too much information which guides them in exactly how to solve whatever problem we are asking them to answer. In real life, he argues, we almost never have exactly the right information delivered to us at exactly the right time. Frequently we have too much information and have to decide what is important for what we want to achieve and what is not. Just as often we have too little information and have to make a decision about what additional information we need and how to go about finding it. Meyer has had an influence on many maths educators by encouraging them to present problems to learners with as little spoon-fed information as possible and allowing them to decide what is important. Sometimes we are just too helpful and provide learners with such closely delivered support as to hamper their efforts to develop problem-solving strategies. Worse still, we may provide so much support that it is actually distracting students from the process they are trying to work through.

All of this relates to the fourth principle of Gancarz's philosophy, that *a system should be designed to assume that its users know what they are doing.* People who are new to a system often find it confusing and hard to learn – it has not been designed to guide them through the way it works, so they have to make a conscious effort to learn how to get things done. This means it takes a while to get going with it, but the payback is that they have got into good habits for learning the next

---

4 D. Meyer, Math Class Needs a Makeover [video] (2010). Available at: www.ted.com/talks/dan_meyer_math_curriculum_makeover.html.

steps, and the ones after that, and can continue learning and developing in their use without hitting a wall. Sometimes providing less support and feedback can result in more learning.

Imagine what would happen if when you asked a question you met the answer with silence. The result could be similar to providing thinking time before choosing a member of the class to answer. When hands go up, teachers usually pick the learner who put their hand up straight away. In this way you are most likely picking the person who knew the answer already. Providing time for all students to think before choosing who to answer results in more thinking for more students; the process of answering the question moves from a test of who knows what already to who can think through what the answer might be. Clearly, this depends significantly on the nature of the original question. Better still, using the 'no hands up' approach (discussed in Chapter 5) ensures that everyone has to think as they do not know who is going to be asked to answer.

Responding to an answer with silence leaves more space for thinking. An immediate response from the teacher praising the correctness, or not, of the answer gives no time for the rest of the class to consider what they think, whether they agree or disagree with the answer and why. It also gives the responder some time to expand their response, to question themselves or consider it in more detail.

Leaving space can be a powerful teaching tool throughout all age ranges. Whilst working with a class, it is customary to have a monologue going on about what they are doing, how they are responding and what stage their learning is at; it is all part of the constant monitoring, adapting and intervening that teachers do. However, sometimes it can be more effective not to share this with the class and instead give them some space and silence to work things out for themselves.

Many Early Years teachers are very good at this. When working with young children, for whom every activity is potentially a new experience, it is tempting to give an almost running commentary of questions and responses as you monitor how they are engaging with an activity. Unfortunately, this can easily lead to over-supporting and taking over. Children need space to think and problem solve; an adult-led commentary on everything they do can take away this space – leading to dependence. When children are stuck, some of the best Early Years teachers leave them to it, giving them breathing space to think the problem through whilst the teacher observes and considers what the barrier might be. This not only gives the children time to think, but it also gives the teacher time to formulate a response which can support them to move to a solution rather than simply telling them what to do. Silence is golden. If it is to be broken, then aim to do so only with equally valuable input – a key question or observation is often all that is needed to push students on to the next step and let them get on with it.

Many of us find it difficult to step back from the standard responses, particularly praising every correct, or even close to correct, answer we receive. The 'well done' impulse is almost hard-wired in us, and quite often it is used as an acknowledgement of any response almost regardless of its content. Pause for a moment and think about how you respond when questioning. Consider how often the response you give is some kind of praise for giving an answer rather than an engagement with the content of the answer. If 'well done' does become tantamount to a verbal tick, then it might be more meaningful to replace it with 'OK' or some other form of acknowledgement rather than praise.

In his provocatively titled *Punished by Rewards*, Alfie Kohn discusses the problems inherent in praise, citing a number of studies which have shown that praise actually decreases student performance.[5] He casts praise as a force that often erodes children's intrinsic motivation and makes them

---

5 A. Kohn, *Punished by Rewards: The Trouble with Gold Stars, Incentive Plans, A's, Praise, and Other Bribes* (New York: Houghton Mifflin, 1999).

dependent on their teachers. That is certainly not to say that feedback is undesirable, but if it is simply positive feedback for providing some kind of response, no matter what the quality of that response, then we need to consider what kind of message it is giving. This is a complex issue as there are such huge variables in the way praise is given. As Kohn observes, a small change in the inflection of the voice when making a statement of praise can also make a significant difference in how it is perceived. However, to praise *any* response in a positive way can send the message that what is acceptable in this class, with this teacher, is any answer the students care to give. A very different message is given if the response to a lacklustre answer and one that is really well thought through are noticeably different.

Another dangerous possibility with overzealous responses to learners is what Doug Lemov calls 'rounding up'.[6] This is the tendency of teachers to accept a basic answer from a learner and, rather than making them work it up into a better one, providing the extra detail and analysis needed for them to take it further. For example, a teacher might ask a class why we experience night and day and receive the answer 'because the Earth spins'. In some senses this is correct but it misses some crucial details, but a teacher rounding up might respond that it was correct and then go on to add the detail that this is because the Earth's surface spins from facing the sun and being bathed in light to turning away and being dark. The problem is that the learner was spared the effort and thinking needed to refine their correct but limited answer into one that was of the required depth. It is very easy to fall into this trap, particularly if you have a certain level of detail in mind when asking a question. Instead of rounding up, it can be more challenging and effective to ask the responder if they are able to elaborate on their answer rather than assuming that this is the level of their understanding and moving on. Silence is golden, so holding back from rounding up their responses and

---

6 D. Lemov, *Teach Like a Champion: 49 Techniques That Put Students on the Path to College* [audio CD] (San Francisco, CA: John Wiley & Sons, 2009).

simply asking for more can make a significant difference to the level of thinking taking place in a classroom.

Just as the Unix philosophy makes the assumption that little feedback is needed for those who know what they are doing, expecting learners to demonstrate they know what they are doing can make a difference to the thinking that is expected of them. The result of expecting students to know what they are doing is that, if they do not, they are put in a position where they must take responsibility for working it out. This is not to say that teachers should not be teaching young people and providing them with new knowledge and with answers, but often a few extra moments of silence can make all the difference between thoughtful engagement and development of thinking, and setting the expectation of them as passive receivers who know that not making the effort leads to them getting the answers anyway.

Saying less to encourage more learning might at first appear counterintuitive, but it is this very contrariness that encourages us to think differently about how things happen in the classroom. This takes us to the final principle of the Unix philosophy I am going to consider – one that seems so counterintuitive that it provides another powerful counterpoint to how we think about learning. This is the idea that *worse is better*, a phrase originally coined by Richard P. Gabriel to describe an approach to software design that favours practicality over functionality or perfection.

Software design is in many ways a very logical pursuit, and when constructing anything that follows very strict or logical rules the temptation is often to strive for perfection. After all, if you follow the rules and solve inconsistencies then surely you will have something that can be deemed perfect. In artistic endeavours, which are usually more complex and messy, there is more of an acceptance that perfection can never be reached.

Worse is better is an attempt to prevent this; rather than working towards what is perfect, you work towards what works. Perfection takes a huge amount of time, but workable solutions come a lot quicker and can therefore be more useful; they are working in the field long before the perfect is even finished. Also, aiming for perfection often involves setting things up in certain ways to support that ultimate end, which can be less effective in the short term.

Worse is better provides an interesting perspective on teaching and learning, as this is another area where we often focus on what could be perfect. This is obviously for different reasons than the pursuit of logical perfection engaged in by programmers and software designers; there are few things less logical than the differing ways that students learn. In the case of teaching, this drive for perfection is often because we know what we are doing is desperately important, and so deserves to be as perfect as possible.

This can lead to a number of issues, the first and most obvious being that striving for perfection is exhausting in many fields, let alone a job as complex and demanding as teaching. Aiming to make every aspect of your practice perfect often results in late nights planning and preparing, skipped lunch breaks to do the same or fix last-minute issues, and the often inevitable burnout before the term is out that leaves you limping into the holidays and, more importantly, being less than effective in the final weeks of terms. Early in my teaching career, I was lucky to work with a manager who was of the opinion that it was better to be less organised and more rested and fresh than the other way around, so I swapped the late-night planning sessions for making sure I got plenty of sleep. This had two notable effects. Firstly, I was more refreshed and so dealt with the delivery of my lessons and engagement with my classes more effectively. Also I was generally in a better frame of mind.

After a while it also had a more subtle effect. The problem with late-night working sessions is that once you have committed to the late night and lack of sleep, it appears that you have a huge amount of time at your disposal. Couple that with being less focused and efficient due to being tired, and you have a recipe for taking far longer than needed to get anything done. Setting a realistic deadline that ensures you get a good amount of sleep reduces the time available, so faced with a shorter deadline I found that I was more purposeful in getting things done. I also concentrated on what was most important about planning, and focused on those key aspects rather than getting caught up in details.

Another issue with striving for perfection in education is the fact that we all have our own varying, but usually equally strong, ideas about what perfection actually means. As discussed in Chapter 2, education is inherently ideological, and most teachers have a very robust concept of what they believe education should look like. The problem with this is that there can be a significant divide between what we want education to look like in a perfect world and what is actually most effective within the context of our day-to-day teaching. Your notion of perfect might be just right for a child who is growing up in a context similar to your own, it might even be just the thing for a child in a different environment if certain factors were different, but it is often not going to be right for the students you actually teach.

I grew up in a middle-class area; there was never any question about whether I would go to school every day or whether I would have the support and material things I needed to be able to engage well with school. School gave me the basics, although in areas such as reading and writing my parents had already started me off and continued to support me. At home I was given the space to take on my own projects, from recording 'radio shows' with a cassette recorder to playing and writing music. This time and space constituted a huge part of my learning, and hence, when I became a teacher, I placed a strong emphasis on children's own choices and interests leading pathways for learning. For me, this was such an important part of growing up that it underpinned my own ideology of education.

When I started looking for my first teaching job, I found this thinking challenged when I visited a school in London. This was an all-through academy in an area of high deprivation with an unusual approach to depth and breadth. Children came into the primary school significantly below national expectations in their knowledge and skills. To tackle this, the primary phase was strongly focused on the core skills of literacy and numeracy to the exclusion of the kind of cross-curricular, project-based learning I had been trying to develop in my own practice. The curriculum broadened when the children reached the secondary phase, but the head teacher put to me the argument that there was little point in trying to give breadth beyond a certain point if the children were unable to read and write and therefore access the curriculum.

As a new teacher looking to develop my own ideology of teaching and learning, this was not the right job for me, but it was hard to argue with their outcomes. The school was producing excellent results and opening up opportunities for children from backgrounds that would have left many of them struggling in the face of a more mainstream approach to schooling. If more of these children had extra support at home with their reading then maybe more cross-curricular learning would have broadened their horizons. For a whole variety of reasons – from lack of English skills, resources or just time – the majority of them did not, and to try to provide them with a middle-class influenced vision of what school should be would have risked them missing out on the skills they needed to give them the best opportunities.

This particular school was quite some distance from what I deemed to be 'perfect', yet they were adopting an approach to teaching and learning which aimed to have the maximum impact on the community of children they were there to serve. Whilst this may have been 'worse', in the sense of fitting with my ideology of what education should look like, it was 'better' than what I would have wanted to do with them in terms of outcomes for the children.

Whilst education is very high stakes and we are right to want to aim for the perfect, each group of learners that comes into a school only has one chance at it. The concept of 'worse is better' invites us to question whether our children might be best served by an approach that is designed for them in terms of practicalities and outcomes, even if it strays from our personal notions of what a perfect education might be. As Gabriel's and Gancarz's observations suggest, it is sometimes better for education to be simple and effective than to be 'correct'; and in matters of providing the best opportunities for young people, it is arguably better to aim for impact than for our own notions of perfection.

There are many lessons to be learned from taking values that have emerged from a very different context, such as computer software, and applying them to how we think about teaching and learning. In fact, it is this very difference that can provide such interesting perspectives to contrast with how we normally do things. The main work of software design involves taking logical systems and exploring how they can best work when combined with the illogical and complex situations created by their users. The best software is designed around the needs of these users, and companies with a focus on usability have seen enormous success from carefully considering the requirements and experiences of the individuals using their products. Alongside all of the smaller contrasts and lessons from the IT world, it is the notion of thinking through each and every decision from the perspective of the end user that can give the best insights for the thinking teacher.

Chapter 10

Learning as becoming

Much is made of the legacy of the Industrial Revolution for our school systems – the very notion of schools as institutions for the masses arguably comes from this time. Often it is the physical concept of schools as large institutions with attendance for all, rather than the privileged few, which is seen to be the most important of these legacies. Sometimes it is the smaller details, such as the layout of school buildings and classrooms, the rows of desks and teacher-centric organisation. In more critical circles, it is often the discipline, the control and the preparation of young people for a heavily structured working life.

To me, it is something else, something which underpins the whole way we think about learning and consequently all of the work we do as teachers. This legacy is so great precisely because we do *not* regularly talk about it; it is largely unquestioned and inherent in our thinking. This is the metaphor of learning as a tangible product – we acquire this as we learn, ticking off the boxes as we attain each new skill or body of knowledge.

We think in metaphors, constantly relating one idea to another like the physical connections in our brains. As I just did, one concept is likened to another in order for us to visualise and understand it, but sometimes particular metaphors become so ingrained that we no longer realise that they are metaphors. This is fine as long as they aid our thinking, but sometimes they can actually constrain the way we think.

We are prone to using metaphors from the physical world for things that are more conceptual: communication is often conceived as the delivery and receipt of messages, like letters; energy is envisaged as something that is consumed, like food (even though physics tells us it is also conserved). Often these simplifications help us to concentrate on the most important matters and ignore others.

Learning is no different: we have built whole systems and vocabulary on the idea that learning is like the process of acquiring physical objects. Qualifications and certificates are collected once you have demonstrated that you have produced certain work or acquired certain knowledge or skills from given criteria. A lesson is successful if you have reached the objective, and you succeed in a particular course if you stockpile all of these objectives. When we reach an understanding, we 'get' it – we 'possess' understanding. Likewise, we 'build' learning or 'receive' it. If we do not 'get' something then we are 'lacking' – there is a 'gap' in our understanding, like a space caused by missing bricks in a wall. Learning is framed as a process of acquiring knowledge or skills as things we keep, take with us and use in the future, or not as the case may be.

A paper from the late 1990s by Anna Sfard labels this underlying metaphor as the 'acquisition metaphor'.[1] Once revealed as a metaphor, it becomes clear that this is not the only way of seeing things and she suggests a possible alternative – the 'participation metaphor'.

Rather than acquiring a certain set of skills, accumulating a collection of knowledge or ticking off a list of criteria, the participation metaphor suggests thinking about learning as becoming someone, like a member of a particular community. This is not about a specific list of skills or knowledge, although clearly members of certain communities know and do certain things. It is more about being able to operate as a member of that community – a metaphor that comes more readily to certain types of learning than others, particularly learning in the workplace.

---

1 A. Sfard, On Two Metaphors for Learning and the Dangers of Choosing Just One, *Educational Researcher* 27(2) (1998): 4–13. Available at: edr.sagepub.com/content/27/2/4.

Apprenticeships – whether formal qualifications or informal inductions to a particular job – are an obvious example. When you are inducted into a workplace community, you are taught certain skills or sets of knowledge, but you also learn to operate in that environment, to use the conventions and language of the place, and to interact with the people who inhabit it. Depending on how this process is set up, it can be more about 'becoming one of the team' than gaining the knowledge you need. One of the key works in this area is Étienne Wenger's *Communities of Practice*, which was originally based on an analysis of learning amongst a group of insurance claims processors.[2] His study of the experience of settling into a new job is a useful example of learning as induction rather than the acquisition of a specific set of objects.

The metaphor of participation is a flexible way of thinking about continuing learning rather than learning having an end point. A member of a team can be effective without knowing everything there is to know in an area; part of this is about their confidence in participating in that particular field. They continue to learn as they go, and perhaps even reach the stage of becoming an expert. In the world outside of school, being an expert is often more about how you are perceived rather than any particular knowledge or qualifications; it is about who you are and how you behave.

This metaphor is more readily applied at the end point of formal education – when you become a graduate, an engineer, a doctor or a teacher. These identities imply knowing and being able to perform certain skills, but they are about more than simply a list of attributes. You could learn every one of the specific standards required of teachers in the UK, but it is the act of doing that leads to you calling yourself a teacher. If you were performing the role in a school you would describe yourself as a teacher; if you were unemployed but searching for a job you would also describe yourself as a teacher; but if you had gained a PGCE and then

---

2 É. Wenger, *Communities of Practice: Learning, Meaning, and Identity* (Cambridge: Cambridge University Press, 1998).

gone on to work full time in retail, you might no longer describe yourself as a teacher.

However, learning as becoming does not just apply to vocational or academic courses. Learning to read, for example, first involves the acquisition of a specific set of knowledge about the letter sounds of the alphabet, words and their meanings. At primary school, it becomes much more complex, and more about participation in a society which reads, interprets and discusses certain constructs, such as stories and narratives, and draws meaning from them. This is not a case of piling up interpretation after interpretation until you have a big enough collection; it is about becoming someone who reads and interprets for themselves. This is the difference between a young child who 'can read' and a person who is 'literate'. In reality, we do not always switch from one state of being to another; sometimes multiple states continue to exist; others wax and wane. The participation metaphor for learning is about action rather than possession. We do not collect certain states like badges of belonging, rather we exist in that way for a period of time.

One of the difficulties with the acquisition metaphor, which is so prevalent in the way we currently discuss learning, is that it is quite straightforward to measure that learning. Measuring what people have is easy to understand, if not always easy to achieve, but it is possible. Measuring what people have become is rather more difficult, particularly at any level of detail. You can tell whether someone is a member of a certain community by observing them, but deciding how far away someone is from achieving a precise goal, or knowing what they need to do to guarantee getting a specific job, is rather more difficult. When using the acquisition metaphor, you can measure what someone has without much involvement from them. You can look for evidence to tick off or set a test in which they must demonstrate the knowledge and skills they possess. Measuring who someone is, or who they have become, is conceptually much more difficult, as it is as much about the perceptions they have inside as what they display on the outside.

We are so invested in the acquisition metaphor that it is difficult to begin to consider school through the lens of the participation metaphor; it requires a significant rethink of the purpose of education. If school is about becoming someone then we need to ask who and what that person is. It is easy to look only to the next level: nursery is about becoming a primary school pupil, primary school is about becoming a secondary school student and so on. If this is the case, then we would probably benefit from significantly more communication between these stages of schooling, although this is far from the only argument for this development.

Like most big questions about education, this thinking leads us back to the question: what is the purpose of education? It might be coming full circle, but considering what this means in terms of what people become, rather than what they gain, brings a very different perspective to the debate. In terms of induction and behaviours in school, we often concentrate on producing successful students who are able to operate productively in the school environment. If this is the main focus of learning as becoming then it may be rather lacking – after all, as soon as the student leaves school they no longer need to be the person they have become. Perhaps, instead, we need to focus on what becoming an educated person might mean. Whilst this might seem rather vague, its vagueness could, in fact, be a strength in that it encourages us to think more deeply about what being educated means, rather than what becoming a person with a certain job means.

This raises questions about what it feels like to be an educated person – how such a person behaves and interacts with others and the world – rather than what they have. Someone who is educated in the field of mathematics and someone who is educated in the field of fine art, for example, is going to base their identity on very different ways of knowing and very different processes of doing. So, what is it that makes them educated?

Rather than a set of attributes we can tick off and measure, perhaps it is the way they approach life that makes them educated. Whilst this may be much harder to evaluate than whether they have achieved a particular set of criteria, it goes some way towards addressing the problem of learning post-school. If it is about what you become, then it matters not whether you 'use' what you learned in school, but rather whether you continue to be what you became, or even use this to become someone different.

The big question is, if you were to shift your thinking from learning as acquiring to learning as becoming, how would your teaching change? This shift transforms a subject from a collection of knowledge or skills to be gained, to a field of discussion, a community and a space. A classroom based around students becoming participants in the subject rather than possessors of certain, closely defined slices of it, could potentially look and feel very different. Certainly, knowledge would have to be used and skills demonstrated, but the primary focus would be participation in the subject – asking the kinds of questions that people in that field ask and doing the kinds of things they do.

This sounds potentially like an argument for 'learning by doing' – for the notion of 'experiential learning' that John Dewey,[3] David Kolb[4] and many others have promoted. In a sense it is, but the concept of 'learning as becoming' is not just about doing, but about participating. Students can learn about science from experience, by carrying out pre-planned experiments that their teacher has set, but this is arguably not participation in the scientific field. To do that, students need to carry out the kinds of processes that scientists do – to ask questions and experiment to find answers, to sometimes have experiments that are unsuccessful or lead to nothing.

---

3 Dewey, *Experience and Education*.

4 D. A. Kolb, *Experiential Learning: Experience as the Source of Learning and Development* (Englewood Cliffs, NJ: Financial Times/Prentice Hall, 1983).

To be fair, this sounds a lot like much current science teaching, although the question to raise is whether this is planned and presented as 'learning questioning skills' or 'becoming a scientist'. This might be a subtle distinction, but it can make a big difference to the way knowledge is perceived. The ownership of 'teaching questioning skills' resides with the teacher, whereas the ownership of any process of becoming is with the person who is doing.

Participating in a subject does not have to mean always carrying out activities that have some loose link to the subject content or require you to use some of the accepted skills. What it means is more fully entering the field and doing what practitioners in that field do. For example, we could make learning about Tudor monarchs more active by setting up some sort of problem-solving treasure hunt, an activity which, if designed carefully, could also involve history skills. However, this is still not what the work of history involves: working as a historian involves reading, writing, critical discussion, asking particular types of questions and making links between different areas of knowledge.

There is a vast difference between learning some French and becoming a French speaker. Conditioned as we are to quantify learning, the concept of becoming can seem woolly. Yet as much as we quantify aspects of a subject, we know that most students do not acquire all of the learning set out before them, and instead take some aspects and make them into their own unique understandings. Repositioning the aim of subject teaching in schools as an experience of becoming a member of an intellectual community is highly ambitious. Becoming a musician, a writer or a sportsperson are all greater aims than simply acquiring some knowledge or skills in these areas.

In her paper, Sfard acknowledges that it is unlikely we will completely replace the acquisition metaphor with the participation one, but it is possible to use both depending on the circumstances. However, even opening our minds to there being another metaphor that we could use reveals how ingrained the idea of learning as collecting is – and how significantly differently we could see what we do if we took the time to think about learning as becoming.

Chapter 11

On inspiration

We are all capable of making things happen and, on rare occasions, of doing great things, sometimes things that amaze even ourselves. This is hard. Transforming an idea into a reality takes time – the blank page takes enormous effort to fill. Getting started on something new is notoriously difficult, even though we know that we are capable of achieving a lot. Once started, the process can start to feel easier, but often obstacles and day-to-day pressures can grind you down. At such times there is often a sense that something is missing; it feels very different from when you have momentum and are moving forward. What you need is inspiration.

Teachers have to deliver on a huge number of ideas. We are often constantly switching between different blocks of subject matter, or even subjects, looking for new ways to present the material that will be most effective for our classes, and adapting to new initiatives. Increasingly, teachers are turning to online networks to discuss their practice and share ideas – posting blogs reflecting on that successful lesson, sharing ideas on Twitter and posting videos that influence them on Facebook. Everywhere you look on social media you see inspiration. A TED talk, a quote, a forthcoming conference – the most important attribute seems to be that they profess to be inspiring.

Being inspired feels good; it makes you feel energised and that you are capable of taking the next step and moving on. The trouble is that the effect wears off quite quickly – in a way that is unrelated to any action we may or may not have taken as a result of that initial inspiration. So, back we go to Twitter or TED for another quick hit of encouragement, another dose of enthusiasm, to make us feel that we can be as powerful as we thought we were when riding that inspiration peak.

The natural way of things is for that initial inspiration to kick off a project which we continue to work on to fruition. The pleasant feeling of inspiration can then be replaced by the feeling of achievement, and that, in itself, can often be inspiration enough for the next project or goal. Unfortunately, achieving anything that is worthwhile rarely happens in this way. More often than not, there are challenges to overcome, holes that appear in the original idea and spaces that need to be plugged in order to make it work. All of these can lead to frustration and certainly require hard work. The danger is that with such vast amounts of inspiring material only a click (or a touch) away that we get hooked on the inspiration high without ever actually getting on with making a real difference.

Inspiration is a tricky fellow. Nate Kornell and colleagues recently conducted some research which showed that when material was delivered by a charismatic presenter, with the affectations of many so-called 'inspiring speakers', the students felt they had learnt more than with a less engaging teacher, even though the content was the same.[1] The study found that the slick and 'inspiring' presentation style of TED talks played havoc with some people's perceptions of what they had learned, making them overestimate the effectiveness of their learning. In some cases, it seems, a dose of inspiration does wonders for speakers' feedback forms, but actually deceives the learners. Just think about that: by billing that speaker or talk as 'inspiring' you might inadvertently be branding them as an artist of deception!

---

1 S. K. Carpenter, M. M. Wilford, N. Kornell and K. M. Mullaney, Appearances Can Be Deceiving: Instructor Fluency Increases Perceptions of Learning Without Increasing Actual Learning, *Psychonomic Bulletin and Review* (May 2013). Available at: link.springer.com/article/10.3758/s13423-013-0442-z.

Another danger with inspiration is that it sends you off on tangents. Regularly seeking out new ideas can have a positive effect on what you are doing, but too regularly and we can end up switching from one thing to another without ever mastering anything. Professor Dylan Wiliam puts this well when he describes teachers as being like magpies[2] – we have all heard teachers talking about 'magpie-ing', 'borrowing' or 'stealing' ideas. Wiliam says that this can be dangerous even when sharing good practice between schools, because sharing good ideas often ends up as a case of trying one idea after the next and becoming a distraction from refining and mastering the things that we are doing already. What makes a real difference to learning are the things we do every day and become a habit, not the one-off episodes we try before moving on to the next novel idea. Building these habits takes time, but constantly looking to keep things fresh by seeking out inspiring new ideas undermines this hard work.

So, what are we to do about inspiration? One solution could be to cut down on the diet of inspiration. Rather than seeking its cosy glow, it might be more beneficial to set key actions to carry out and objectives to achieve. This sounds a lot drier than seeking to be effortlessly propelled along by enthusiasm, but it is hard work of this nature that often gets things happening.

Whenever we are feeling inspired by a new idea, it might help to stop for a moment and ask what action we might actually take and whether there is anything constructive that we can do with the idea, or if it is giving us a false sense of what we have learned. If there are positive actions,

---

2 Professor Dylan Wiliam at the Schools Network Annual Conference [video] (2011). Available at: www.youtube.com/watch?v=wKLo15A80lI.

then find time to get on with them. If there aren't, then it is just another dose of the intangible glow of inspiration that isn't magically going to make something happen. We all need a bit of good feeling in our work, but perhaps we should be aiming for achievement not inspiration.

Chapter 12

Don't settle

You've got to find what you love, and that is as true for work as it is for your lovers. … If you haven't found it yet, keep looking, and don't settle. As with all matters of the heart, you'll know when you find it, and like any great relationship it just gets better and better as the years roll on. So keep looking. Don't settle.

Steve Jobs[1]

So said the founder of Apple in his commencement address to graduating students at Stanford University. We often talk with young people about the importance of having high standards and cultivating the outlooks displayed by highly successful people like Jobs — one of the most renowned perfectionists of the modern business world. Yet setting such ambitious goals does not always sit well with some of our cultural norms about valuing contributions whatever they are, of trying our best and being content with what we achieve. The balance between ambition and contentment is a problematic one, and the conflict comes across in the different messages we give to young people. When is it best to aim for the stars and when should you decide to settle?

Apart from the occasional happy accident due to extremely favourable circumstances (or talent), great achievements are rarely reached by setting less-than-great goals. There is a tendency for us to stop when we reach the destination we expect and for that to become normal. This level of achievement can then become the benchmark we aim for in the future.

---

1 S. Jobs, Transcript of Commencement Speech at Stanford given by Steve Jobs (2005). Available at: www.freerepublic.com/focus/chat/1422863/posts.

James Rhem writes about 'self-fulfilling prophecies' when he recounts the story of the Hollerith tabulating machine, which was used by the US Census Bureau in the late nineteenth century.[2] Its inventor estimated workers could use the machine to process 550 cards a day, and once they had got to grips with the machine they did so. They even managed to improve on this figure, but not without significant effort and at 'great emotional cost'. So, when a greater workload needed to be dealt with, more employees were hired. These workers had not been told of the current performance rate and proceeded to process 2,100 cards per day without problems. Their lack of normalised expectations led to them being over 280 per cent more productive. Clearly, there are limits and setting a target of 4,000 cards per day may well have hit the ceiling of what was possible, but this study shows the significant difference to outcomes that goals and perceptions of achievement can create.

Setting high standards for ourselves and striving to be the best we can be are notions that are enshrined in the rhetoric of most schools. Across the world, youngsters are encouraged to set their goals high. The implication is that you are unlikely to achieve higher than your sights are set, so setting them high means you will not be limited by an unrealistically low expectation of yourself. Young people are encouraged to live by the example of sporting heroes, great figures from history and contemporary overachievers, like Jobs. Yet the high aspirations instilled during an assembly, for example, are often tempered at other times by the message that what we should aim for is the best that we are capable of, rather than the best that we can imagine.

Implicit in the message of 'all you can do is your best' – that it can be acceptable to reach a less-than-perfect outcome if the effort that has gone into it is the best you could give – is that your expectations should be regulated and realistic; that it is all right never to be the best as long as you are the best that *you* can be. This message is logical; after all, the

---

2 J. Rhem, Pygmalion in the Classroom (n.d.). Available at: cte.udel.edu/sites/udel.edu.cte/files/ntlf/v8n2/pygmalion.htm.

commitment required for a high level of success makes it difficult for everyone to excel in every area. It is also logical for the more difficult to swallow reason that most people will never truly excel in any area. Tempering high self-expectations to avoid bitter disappointment makes sense, then, but is a problematic partner to the messages we give around setting high expectations for success.

The initial group of workers on the Hollerith tabulating machine set their expectations and then worked to them. Acting above this threshold caused them considerable difficulty and stress, yet their colleagues without such compromised expectations were able to significantly outstrip them without experiencing these problems.

Aiming for the best you can be, rather than the top, also involves defining what you think you are capable of; you cannot know if you have reached a certain level of effort if you have not defined what it is. Unfortunately, setting a benchmark can be problematic in itself. Psychologist Carol Dweck has spent her career producing a body of research demonstrating the problems that emerge when we have a strong definition of our capabilities.[3] She defines the state of believing that you have a set capability as a 'fixed mindset'. This type of attitude is reinforced by many things, from IQ tests giving a flat score of intelligence to some instances of grouping by ability in schools which are rigid and inflexible. Clearly, this is not always the thinking behind structures such as streaming, but what is important is the way they are perceived; if no one ever moves between groups then there is a clear perception that individuals have a fixed level of achievement. Likewise, if people do move between sets, but it is framed as them being in 'the wrong group', then the movement simply acts as a correction to an error, which again reinforces this fixed concept of ability.

---

3 C. Dweck, *Mindset: How You Can Fulfil Your Potential* (New York: Random House, 2012).

Dweck has found that the perception of fixed ability makes people less likely to achieve. Those with 'growth mindsets', however, who believe that their capabilities are not fixed and they can improve, have been found to be much more successful in a whole range of situations and measures. Dweck's findings are not based on formal assessments of an individual's capabilities, but on their own perceptions; simply believing that you can develop makes it more likely that you will.

Whilst the message that young people should not settle and aim as high as they want might logically appear to be setting them up for failure, if it is nuanced with the notion that they are able to develop their capabilities and that they are not fixed, then it could directly contribute to their success. Conversely, the message that it is acceptable to do the best that you can, regardless of the outcome, potentially sets up the very 'fixed mindset' that Dweck has found to hold people back.

There is an implicit assumption in this discussion which is that it is desirable to be highly successful. On the face of it this seems like a strange thought – much of our society, and particularly the mainstream media, is built around celebrating success. However, the biographies of many famous people often make for interesting reading precisely because they are not the kind of lives many of us would like to live ourselves. Success requires a determination, focus and dedication that is hard to achieve and often subsumes an individual's entire life. Whether sportspeople, politicians, entrepreneurs or musicians, the highly successful personalities we look up to often have a lifestyle that involves a huge amount of hard work and sacrifice.

Tim Bergen is one of the world's most successful DJs and dance music artists, who seemingly came out of nowhere. With an iTunes number one single that received relentless radio play, he now DJs around 250 nights a year to crowds of tens of thousands, and is allegedly worth

US$7 million.[4] After being spotted by promoter Ash Pournouri for his talent for writing a catchy melody, the pair produced hundreds of tracks to find the blueprint for success. They analysed the music that was successful for other people, tirelessly and systematically developing a formula for tracks that would work both on the dance floor and the radio, and which would propel them to global stardom. Having mastered this, Bergen spent 18 months learning to DJ before building up a schedule of playing gigs across the world. He now travels from country to country, away from home most of the time, with a schedule of gigs so relentless it has put him in hospital at least once.

'Coming out of nowhere', it seems, takes a seed of potential and an awful lot of very focused hard work to learn what is needed to get to the top, and then to stay there. The trappings of being highly successful might look very attractive, and the kind of hard work it takes may be a laudable goal to aspire to, but how many people would want the realities of that life? Choosing a career path is usually painted as being about the job itself, but with many careers, particularly at a high level, it is as much about the lifestyle that the job imposes. Perhaps this is another factor behind why we encourage young people to aim for the top but also temper their aspirations: being at the top might not be a very pleasant experience. You only have to look back at those celebrity biographies to see the emotional and physical fallout that a life at the top can often entail.

Creating high expectations for ourselves is often complex and fraught with problems, but expectations come not only from within but also from other people. Teachers are well used to the mantra of high expectations for young people, of not settling in their expectations of what the classes they teach can achieve. This seems like a moral issue, an issue of respect; it is only fair to expect that young learners can achieve. Yet many of us will have taught classes where we expected more of

---

4 See Forbes, The World's Highest-Paid DJs (2012). Available at: www.forbes.com/sites/zackomalleygreenburg/2012/08/02/the-worlds-highest-paid-djs/.

certain groups or individuals than they managed to achieve. Whilst we may have a rhetoric of high expectations for all, these are often moderated by our knowledge of the backgrounds, perceived intelligence and experiences of our students.

When we judge that a certain group is going to struggle to achieve in a certain subject, based on our previous experience, this is not something that we would normally communicate to them directly. Why? A series of studies by Rosenthal and Jacobson found that whether teachers choose to settle or not in their expectations of learners actually has considerable bearing on how those pupils achieve.[5] In their famous Oak School experiment, teachers' expectations of their pupils were deliberately manipulated to see if they had an effect on how the children achieved in an IQ test. It was found that the students whom the teachers had been told to expect a higher pace of achievement did achieve higher; the predictions became a self-fulfilling prophecy.

To return to the Steve Jobs quote at the beginning of this chapter, it would appear that his call 'don't settle', and the mindsets that may be adopted by either teachers or learners as a result, can have a significant impact. Expectations may seem like a nebulous force but, whether they come from within or from others, setting high expectations and believing you can achieve them may actually take you some of the way towards getting there.

So far, we have only explored the notion of settling as giving up prematurely. However, as well as the call to setting high expectations, there is another meaning contained in the phrase 'don't settle', which is perhaps more literal: don't settle down, don't get too comfortable, don't keep things the same. In this sense, 'settling down' refers to sticking at one thing, in one place or with one person – something which is usually depicted as being intertwined with success rather than failure.

---

5 R. Rosenthal and D. Jacobson, *Pygmalion in the Classroom: Teacher Expectation and Pupils' Intellectual Development* (Carmarthen: Crown House Publishing, 2003).

Traditionally, settling with one job allowed you to move up the ranks, gain the experience that was necessary for promotion, increase your salary and accrue a pension for your retirement. Settling in one place allowed you to buy a house and watch it rise in value, invest time in friends and family in the local area and carve out a place in the world. Settling with one person was the socially accepted way of starting a family and of taking on socially expected roles.

To differing degrees, all of these things are changing or have changed already. Some have been influenced by technological change: communication and travel are now much cheaper, more accessible and more sophisticated than they were fifty years ago, allowing people to maintain their relationships even if they move away from where they grew up, or take on a more mobile lifestyle. As a result, many of us are moving around considerably more.

In some instances, this has been influenced by economic factors: the cost of mortgages to buy a house has become increasingly prohibitive for young people, and the guarantee of increasing property values looks very uncertain. This may change, but at the moment the result is that increasing numbers of people are delaying or putting off completely the traditional property purchase involved in 'settling down'. Social factors have also played a part – divorce and family breakup have become more common and also more accepted than they once were. Many families defy the traditional image of being 'settled', although this is not a value judgement as many non-traditional families provide the stability and support that children need.

Work is also changing and becoming more globalised. We are able to work from different locations due to communications technologies, which are changing incredibly quickly, and these too are requiring employees to adapt and change. This adaptability is increasingly needed to move through the growing number of portfolio careers that many people have now. In some sectors, experience has become more transferable and it is simply more accepted that an individual may have a number of careers in their lifetime. Although these are often seen to be general trends, is not the case in all industries – I recently saw a job advert for an electrical engineer requiring twenty years of experience in power management systems for specialised computer servers. There are still careers, such as medicine, that are seen as jobs for life due to the expertise that must be built up over time to be successful. However, over all, the world of work is increasingly 'un-settled'.

Whilst many are finding jobs and careers more shifting and uncertain, some people are building a life on the very antithesis of 'settled'. Author Tim Ferris coined the term 'lifestyle design' to describe an approach to work involving using online and mobile businesses to create a working life based around short experiences or 'mini retirements'.[6] This philosophy in echoed in Chris Guillebeau's *The Art of Non-Conformity*,[7] and an increasing number of people are writing online about leveraging the benefits of the unsettled world in which we now live to realise ambitions and live lives of varied experiences rather than saving and hoping for a good retirement.

The flexibility that is now possible means that working for a lifetime to accrue the capital to support ourselves in retirement now makes little sense. When you are tied to one area or one job, you are tied to experiences in that one place rather than being able to take advantage of all the things you wish you could do but can only free yourself up to do during your two weeks of annual leave.

To lifestyle designers like Ferris, the idea of settling in terms of lowering your expectations and staying in one place are inevitably intertwined. Once you settle in the second sense you also settle in the first. So, settling can set people up with low expectations which prevent them from

6 Ferris, *The 4 Hour Work Week*.

7 C. Guillebeau, *The Art of Non-Conformity: Set Your Own Rules, Live the Life You Want and Change the World* (London: Turnaround, 2010).

achieving more. It seems Steve Jobs might have been onto something with his mantra 'don't settle'. However, the fact remains that not everyone thrives on challenge and change; a lot of us like the comfort and stability that comes with settling. Many people would rather not race through life trying to become highly successful in a particular field or to experience everything the world has to offer; they are happier taking their time.

It turns out this may not work in quite the way they think, as whether or not we settle can have a significant effect on our perception of time. Neuroscientist David Eagleman's work into how the brain perceives time suggests that those who stick with the familiar may actually perceive their lives to be shorter.[8] Inspired by a childhood near-death experience during which everything seemed to slow down as he tried to save himself, Eagleman's research has led him to explore the phenomenon of time seeming to go very slowly in such circumstances and fly by in others. It seems that the more familiar a situation or experience is, the less the brain writes down about it.

When we are in familiar situations, we are able to rely on memory for a significant part of our actions. Consider your behaviour when you walk into a supermarket: if it is a shop you have been into before, you already know where the different products are and can walk straight to the egg aisle, for example. However, if it is a store you have not visited before, particularly if it is an unfamiliar chain which has a different layout, you lack the necessary memory and therefore have to think about how to find the right aisle.

This effect is replicated in one of Eagleman's experiments which demonstrates what is known as the 'oddball effect'.[9] Participants are shown a series of images on a screen which all appear for the same amount

---

8 See B. Bilger, Profiles: The Possibilian, *New Yorker* (25 April 2011). Available at: www. newyorker.com/reporting/2011/04/25/110425fa_fact_bilger.

9 See Bilger, Profiles: The Possibilian.

of time. Most of the images are the same, but occasionally they are shown a different picture. When asked to estimate the amount of time that each image appears on the screen, participants consistently perceive that the unfamiliar image appears for longer than the familiar, even though they are displayed for exactly the same amount of time.

What Eagleman's experiments suggest is that our perception of time is inextricably linked to this process of thinking and memory; when we rely on memory time slips by more quickly, but when we are forced to think it goes more slowly. This explains our perception of everlasting days during long summer holidays when we were children; in an unfamiliar world, children have to think a lot more and rely on memory a lot less, so they perceive time passing more slowly. As we get older, however, the world is much more familiar to us so we rely on memory more, hence we perceive time moving faster and experience those days where we did little as flying by. It could therefore be argued that not settling can result in a longer life, as the more unfamiliar experiences you continue to have, the longer you will perceive time to pass.

Teaching is generally a stable job, situated in a specific community and geographic place, and built on a structure of routines – from the rhythm of the day to the academic year. The first concern then, as a teacher, is whether you are making your life shorter by your choice of profession – suddenly the pace of change in education policy and the unpredictability of each new year group might not seem so undesirable! As with many such ideas, it is neither good nor bad, but thinking makes it so – it is what you do with it that makes the difference. This may seem like an argument for making everything as unfamiliar and unsettled as possible, but in school it could actually be used the other way round. The effects of unfamiliarity could be an argument for making every aspect of school as familiar as possible, except for the intended learning. Surrounded by familiar routines that require little thinking, a focus on remarkable learning in the classroom could make it more memorable.

It is common practice, particularly in primary education, to use familiar contexts and backgrounds in order to make new learning meaningful and relevant. Eagleman's research suggests that children might be more likely to remember things if they are presented in an unfamiliar context. The more familiar something is, the more likely we are to use our memory. Framing learning around an unfamiliar context might actually encourage a higher degree of attention and potentially encourage more thinking and the retention of more new memories.

Making things consistently unfamiliar would be quite a challenge – it would take a lot of effort to keep coming up with new ways to present learning. However, Eagleman's work suggests that it may be a useful strategy when trying to encourage learners to remember detailed information. Whilst the difficulty involved in implementation may make it best reserved for particularly important or in-depth learning, this will only serve to increase its impact. Increasing attention by using the unfamiliar could be a powerful tool for teachers to pull out when precise recall is what is most needed.

There is also a broader point to consider here: if seeking out the unfamiliar has so many potential benefits, perhaps we should consider the wider messages we give to young people about settling – not just settling for certain expectations, but settling at all. Schools are some of the most settled institutions in our society, and having sought them out as workplaces we must consider how much this is down to us, as teachers, needing to settle. This suggests that, as a profession, we hold a certain view about the importance of settling that, at the very least, the ideas in this chapter have shown are not for everyone. For some people, not settling could lead to more success, a better fit with the constantly changing world of work and even the perception of a longer life.

Traditionally, not settling down has been seen as an irresponsible and ill thought-out lifestyle choice. It turns out it could be rather smarter than it seems to those of us conditioned by society to think that settling is the way to build a future. Stepping outside of society's expectations can enable us to be amazingly successful. Stepping outside your own expectations for yourself can result in the most fulfilled and even a longer life.

Teachers shape young people's thinking on these crucial issues. Yet we rarely think about how our fundamental assumptions about life affect how we come across, and how we communicate these to the learners we work with. There are ways of framing your life that are very different to the stable career, good salary and a settled existence that teaching offers. We owe it to young people to think through how their perspectives might differ and allow them to frame their lives in the way they choose.

Conclusion

The idea persists that too much thinking might make it impossible for us to feel – as if it weren't already quite plainly apparent that a large and constant amount of thinking may be the only thing that can keep us from destroying each other.

Alain de Botton

Thinking matters. The world is changing at a rapid pace and it requires thinking to keep up, let alone move forward in the way that you want to go. If schools are to be places that truly engage with what the future could be, then they need thinking teachers who are willing to seek out new challenges and ask the questions to which they do not have the answers.

Plenty of questions have been asked and answered before, so young people also need teachers who can give them access to this knowledge that they might use it to build their own. They need teachers who have done some thinking already, partly to give them the shortcuts to the knowledge acquired by those who have gone before, and partly to help them develop the ways of thinking they will need in their own lives.

Some of the perspectives in this book come from areas well outside of education. It may seem subversive to suggest that teaching could be influenced by ideas emerging from business, computing or technology. It may also seem subversive to question some of our assumptions about the purpose of education. This subversion is precisely the point: it provides contrasts to enable us to re-examine the way that teaching and learning happen and move it forward from what is best to what is next. Seeking out these kinds of challenges to what we do is key to moving forward, just as it is key to deciding what you think education is really about and what you are really about – to find and articulate your princi-ples. This book is a start, but the world is full of challenges and contrasts to be found and considered, so keep seeking them out.

Whilst much of this book has concentrated on questions and contrasts in teaching, it is my hope that this process will also be adopted by our students. We could just keep asking them questions to which we know the answers and continuing to reproduce the culture that characterises schools, or we could begin to allow them to build the future (of course, bearing in mind the plentiful learning that exists from the past).

After all the thinking, what matters most is what you do with it. Consid-ering all of these issues is desirable in itself, and there is great importance in satisfying our own drive to learn as teachers, if only for ourselves. However, for most teachers, the reason they are in the job is the stu-dents, and the goal of our thinking should be better learning for them. If you agree with the central premise of this book, then thinking teachers must also be encouraging thinking young people, in exactly the ways that have been explored.

It is my belief that there is no such thing as thinking too much. Thinking shapes decisions, but it is decisions that shape the world. Our decisions define us, and as teachers our decisions also define other people. We should make sure, then, that our decisions are well thought through.

further thinking

Thank you for reading. If you want to know more, give feedback or discuss new ideas or new thinking, then please get in touch. You can find my blog at oliverquinlan.com, and I am on Twitter at **@oliverquinlan**.

To find out more about the thinking that has inspired my thinking, I recommend the following:

Books

N. Postman and **C. Weingartner**, *Teaching as a Subversive Activity* (London: Penguin, 1970)

Despite its age, there is still much to be learned from the challenges in this book. It is a plea to reframe teaching and learning as something which changes the world rather than simply recreates it.

K. Facer, *Learning Futures: Education, Technology and Social Change* (London: Routledge, 2011)

In many ways, Facer takes the arguments from *Teaching as a Subversive Activity* and contextualises them in terms of the social challenges we face today. The depth and clarity of her arguments will make you think differently about the purpose of education in society.

P. Bourdieu and **J.-C. Passeron**, *Reproduction in Education, Culture and Society*, tr. R. Nice (London: Sage, 1990 [1970])

This is undoubtedly a heavy read, but an important one in that it explores how education shapes the future to be very much like the past.

P. Freire, *Pedagogy of the Oppressed* (New York: Penguin, 1970)

A classic piece of thinking on education in which Freire explores how to avoid the reproduction inherent in much education and instead aim for education as true empowerment.

A. S. Neill, *Summerhill* (Harmondsworth: Penguin, 1962)

One of the first books that made me think really differently about how teaching and learning could work. Neill sets out the philosophy behind the well-known radical school of the title. The second half seems very dated now, with its emphasis on Freudian psychology, but it is a fascinating portrait of an educational project that broke away from how things are usually done.

G. Claxton and **B. Lucas**, *New Kinds of Smart: How the Science of Learnable Intelligence is Changing Education* (Maidenhead: Open University Press, 2011)

In an immensely readable and well-researched book, Claxton and Lucas explore case studies and research which suggest ways of reconsidering how we think about intelligence, and the implications of this for teaching and learning.

A. Kohn, *Punished by Rewards: The Trouble with Gold Stars, Incentive Plans, A's, Praise, and Other Bribes* (New York: Houghton Mifflin, 1999)

Kohn takes something so many of us take for granted – that rewards get results – and deconstructs that assumption so systematically that it will leave you questioning everything you think you know about education.

J. Hattie, *Visible Learning: A Synthesis of Over 800 Meta-Analyses Relating to Achievement* (London: Routledge, 2008)

Hattie's work is often used to justify all manner of arguments around education. The ranking system he uses here to rate the impact of educational achievements has been much debated, but, for me, it is the wider arguments he makes that have made me think again about what is important for learning to happen.

D. T. Willingham, *Why Don't Students Like School: A Cognitive Scientist Answers Questions About How the Mind Works and What It Means for the Classroom* (San Francisco, CA: Jossey Bass, 2009)

Willingham writes in such a way that you come away with a huge insight into how learning works that suddenly seems like total common sense.

S. Godin, *Linchpin: Are You Indispensable? How to Drive Your Career and Create a Remarkable Future* (London: Piatkus, 2010)

This is Godin's rallying cry to rethink our position in society and the agency that we have to shape our lives.

M. Gladwell, *Outliers: The Story of Success* (London: Penguin, 2008)

The '10,000 hours' argument has been cited to death, but it is only one of many models in this book that encourage you to rethink your preconceptions about success. Gladwell has an incredible talent for deconstructing how things work and presenting them as compelling and thought-provoking stories.

M. Krogerus and **R. Tschäppeler**, *The Decision Book: Fifty Models for Strategic Thinking* (London: Profile Books, 2011)

Straightforward methods you can action tomorrow for exploring different ways of thinking about decision-making.

O. Osterwalder and **Y. Pigneur**, *Business Model Generation* (Hoboken, NJ: John Wiley & Sons, 2010)

Breaks down the way businesses work into a neat and straightforward canvas. A must for anyone from a non-business background who is trying to understand business thinking.

T. Kelley, *The Ten Faces of Innovation* (London: Profile Books, 2008)

Kelley seeks to identify the ten different ways of thinking required for innovation. Whilst this comes from a product and design perspective, it is a great example of deliberately viewing the world through different lenses.

C. Leadbeater, *We Think: Mass Innovation Not Mass Production* (London: Profile Books, 2010)

If I were to choose one book on the impact new technologies have had on our lives this would be it. A concise and readable but deeply researched exploration of how technology has made us look again at the way we understand our world.

C. Guillebeau, *The Art of Non-Conformity: Set Your Own Rules, Live the Life You Want and Change the World* (London: Turnaround, 2010)

Guillebeau systematically challenges much of what we take for granted about the way we live our lives, and encourages a different way of seeing the world.

M. Gancarz, *The Unix Philosophy* (Boston, MA: Butterworth-Heinemann, 1995)

Aside from the lessons I have learned and explored in Chapter 9, this is a fascinating read for anyone with an interest in technology and philosophy.

Blogs

Ewan McIntosh's edu.blogs.com

Ewan's ideas on structuring learning, using ideas from the world of design and his astute observations on teaching and learning have been a big influence on me.

Open Educational Thinkering: dougbelshaw.com/blog

Doug Belshaw's blog covers education, formal and informal learning, new technologies and productivity.

Carl Gombrich: www.carlgombrich.org

Carl leads the fascinating Arts and Sciences course at University College London, and he has challenged my thinking on the place of subjects and disciplines in higher education and beyond.

Donald Clark Plan B: donaldclarkplanb.blogspot.co.uk

Never afraid to challenge or cause controversy, Donald is a voice well worth listening to in the field of educational technology and pedagogy.

Neil Hopkin's Blog: neilhopkin.wordpress.com

As the first head teacher I worked for, Neil shaped my thinking on leadership, teaching and learning. He continues to do so through this insightful blog.

Scenes from the Battleground: teachingbattleground.wordpress.com

The anonymous '**Andrew Old**' is a controversial blogger. His blog is an essential read in challenging and refining my thinking.

The Grinch Manifesto: peteyeomans.wordpress.com

Another blogger not afraid to challenge the status quo, **Pete Yeomans** invites readers to think differently about pedagogy and school management, often drawing contrasts from many different areas.

We Are **Simon Bostock**: wearesimonbostock.net

Simon blogs about learning and technology from a perspective I would never encounter without reading his work. Leftfield, perceptive and insightful, his writing often introduces me to subjects I do not find anywhere else.

PlymUniPrimary: Blogs: blogs.plymuniprimary.com

Many of the students I have worked with at Plymouth University write reflective and insightful blogs about their experiences of education. On many occasions they have made me think again about teaching and learning and prompted me to develop ideas in ways I would not have otherwise. Their blogs are collected here.

Twitter

I would encourage anyone wanting to explore more of the ideas in this book to investigate the world of the educational community on Twitter. There are many people sharing ideas and thinking, as well as debating every educational issue you could think of. Try not to be shy, follow many, jump into conversations that are happening with your ideas and examples, and build a network of people who will support and challenge you. I am of the view that it is best to build your own network, but there are some lists of people I would recommend following at **@oliverquinlan/lists**.

Bibliography

All websites last accessed 24 September 2013.

Alexander, R. (ed.) (2009) *Children, their World, their Education: Final Report and Recommendations of the Cambridge Primary Review*. London: Routledge.

Bilger, B. (2011) Profiles: The Possibilian, *New Yorker* (25 April). Available at: www.newyorker.com/reporting/2011/04/25/110425fa_fact_bilger.

Bourdieu, P. and **Passeron, J.-C.** (1990 [1970]) *Reproduction in Education, Culture and Society*, tr. R. Nice. London: Sage.

Brown, D. (2006) *Tricks of the Mind*. London: Transworld.

Carpenter, S. K., Wilford, M. M., Kornell, N. and **Mullaney, K. M.** (2013) Appearances Can Be Deceiving: Instructor Fluency Increases Perceptions of Learning Without Increasing Actual Learning, *Psychonomic Bulletin and Review* (May). Available at: link.springer.com/article/10.3758/s13423-013-0442-z.

Claxton, G. and **Lucas, B.** (2011) *New Kinds of Smart: How the Science of Learnable Intelligence is Changing Education*. Maidenhead: Open University Press.

Deakin Crick, R., Jelfs, H., Huang S. and **Wang, Q.** (2011) *Learning Futures Evaluation Final Report*. Available at: learningemergence.net/technical-reports-2/learning-futures-evaluation-2011/.

Department for Education (2010) *A Profile of Teachers in England from the 2010 School Workforce Census*. Ref: DFE-RR151. Available at: dera.ioe.ac.uk/11897/1/DFE-RR151.pdf.

Department for Education (2011) *Review of the National Curriculum in England: What Can We Learn from the English, Mathematics and Science Curricula of High-Performing Jurisdictions?* Ref: DFE-RR178. Available at: www.education.gov.uk/publications/standard/publicationDetail/Page1/DFE-RR178.

Dewey, J. (2007 [1938]) *Experience and Education*. New York: Free Press.

Drummond, B., and **Cauty, J.** (1988) *The Manual (How To Have a Number One the Easy Way)*. Available at: www.kirps.com/web/main/resources/music/themanual/.

Dweck, C. (2012) *Mindset: How You Can Fulfil Your Potential*. New York: Random House.

Ernest, P. (1991) *The Philosophy of Mathematics Education*. London: Routledge Falmer.

Facer, K. (2011) *Learning Futures: Education, Technology and Social Change*. London: Routledge.

Ferris, T. (2009) *The 4 Hour Work Week: Escape 9–5, Live Anywhere and Join the New Rich*. New York: Random House.

Ferris, T. (2011) *The 4 Hour Body: An Uncommon Guide to Fat Weight Loss, Incredible Sex and Becoming Superhuman*. London: Vermilion.

Forbes (2012) The World's Highest-Paid DJs. Available at: www.forbes.com/sites/zackomalleygreenburg/2012/08/02/the-worlds-highest-paid-djs/.

Freire, P. (1970) *Pedagogy of the Oppressed*. New York: Penguin.

Gancarz, M. (1995) *The Unix Philosophy*. Boston, MA: Butterworth-Heinemann.

Guillebeau, C. (2010) *The Art of Non-Conformity: Set Your Own Rules, Live the Life You Want and Change the World*. London: Turnaround.

Hattie, J. (2008) *Visible Learning: A Synthesis of Over 800 Meta-Analyses Relating to Achievement*. London: Routledge.

Hopkin, N. (2010) Energising Education, *Neil Hopkin's Blog* (6 December). Available at: neilhopkin.wordpress.com/2010/12/06/energising-education/.

Howard Jones, P. (2009) *Introducing Neuroeducational Research: Neuroscience, Education and the Brain from Contexts to Practice*. London: Routledge.

Jobs, S. (2005) Transcript of Commencement Speech at Stanford given by Steve Jobs. Available at: www.freerepublic.com/focus/chat/1422863/posts.

Kagan, S. (2001) *Kagan Cooperative Learning*. San Clemente, CA: Kagan Publishing.

Kohn, A. (1999) *Punished by Rewards: The Trouble with Gold Stars, Incentive Plans, A's, Praise, and Other Bribes*. New York: Houghton Mifflin.

Kolb, D. A. (1983) *Experiential Learning: Experience as the Source of Learning and Development*. Englewood Cliffs, NJ: Financial Times/Prentice Hall.

Lemov, D. (2009) *Teach Like a Champion: 49 Techniques That Put Students on the Path to College* [audio CD]. San Francisco, CA: John Wiley & Sons.

Martin, R. (2009) *The Design of Business: Why Design Thinking is the Next Competitive Advantage*. Boston, MA: Harvard Business School Publishing.

Maslow, A. H. (1943) A Theory of Human Motivation, *Psychological Review* 50(4): 370–396.

McIntosh, E. (2011) Ewan McIntosh #TEDxLondon: The Problem Finders, *Ewan McIntosh's edu.blogs* (18 September). Available at: edu.blogs.com/edublogs/2011/09/ewan-mcintosh-tedxlondon-the-problem-finders.html.

McIntosh, E. (2011) Fewer Instructions, Better Structures, *Ewan McIntosh's edu.blogs* (18 May). Available at: edu.blogs.com/edublogs/2011/05/fewer-instructions-better-structures.html.

McIntosh, E. (2012) SSAT National Conference: Keynote 12 [video] (7 December). Available at: www.youtube.com/watch?v=vxep72WxQSA.

Meyer, D. (2010) Math Class Needs a Makeover [video] (March). Available at: www.ted.com/talks/dan_meyer_math_curriculum_makeover.html.

Miller, T. (2013) I'm Cory Doctorow and This Is How I Work, *Lifehacker* (4 March). Available at: lifehacker.com/5993401/im-cory-doctorow-and-this-is-how-i-work.

OECD (2009) *PISA 2009 Results: What Students Know and Can Do*. Available at: www.oecd.org/edu/pisa/2009.

Postman, N. and **Weingartner, C.** (1970) *Teaching as a Subversive Activity*. London: Penguin.

Quinlan, O. (2012) Definition, Attribution and 'The Field', *Oliver Quinlan* (29 June). Available at: www.oliverquinlan.com/blog/2012/06/29/definition-attribution-the-field/.

Rhem, J. (n.d.) Pygmalion in the Classroom. Available at: cte.udel.edu/sites/udel.edu.cte/files/ntlf/v8n2/pygmalion.htm.

Robinson, K., with **Facer, K.** and **Waters, M.** (2011) Learning Without Frontiers [video] (16 March). Available at: www.youtube.com/watch?v=-iL4rtDnfts.

Rose, J. (2009) *Independent Review of the Primary Curriculum: Final Report* [Rose Review]. Nottingham: DCSF. Available at: www.education.gov.uk/publications/eOrderingDownload/Primary_curriculum_Report.pdf.

Rosenthal, R. and **Jacobson, D.** (2003) *Pygmalion in the Classroom: Teacher Expectation and Pupils' Intellectual Development*. Carmarthen: Crown House Publishing.

Rushton, K. (2012) Number of Smartphones Tops One Billion, *The Telegraph* (17 October). Available at: www.telegraph.co.uk/finance/9616011/Number-of-smartphones-tops-one-billion.html.

Sagan, C. (1980) *Cosmos*. New York: Random House.

Schon, D. (1987) *Educating the Reflective Practitioner*. Chichester: John Wiley & Sons.

Science Guide (2013) Teach First Top Recruiter (15 July). Available at: www.scienceguide.nl/201307/teach-first-top-recruiter.aspx.

Sfard, A. (1998) On Two Metaphors for Learning and the Dangers of Choosing Just One, *Educational Researcher* 27(2): 4–13. Available at: edr.sagepub.com/content/27/2/4.

Stanford University (2008) Steve Jobs' 2005 Stanford Commencement Address [video]. Available at: www.youtube.com/watch?v=UF8uR6Z6KLc.

Victor, B. (2012) Inventing on Principle [video] (22 February). Available at: www.youtube.com/watch?v=PUv66718DII.

Wenger, É. (1998) *Communities of Practice: Learning, Meaning, and Identity*. Cambridge: Cambridge University Press.

Wiliam, D. (2007) Assessment, Learning and Technology: Prospects at the Periphery of Control. Keynote speech at the 2007 Association for Learning Technology Conference in Nottingham. Available at: www.scribd.com/doc/44566598/null.

Wiliam, D. (2011) Professor Dylan Wiliam at the Schools Network Annual Conference [video]. Available at: www.youtube.com/watch?v=wKLo15A80lI.

Willingham, D. T. (2009) *Why Don't Students Like School: A Cognitive Scientist Answers Questions About How the Mind Works and What It Means for the Classroom*. San Francisco, CA: Jossey Bass.

Willingham, D. T. (2009) Why Don't Students *Like* School? Because the Mind Is Not Designed for Thinking, *American Educator* (Spring): 4–13. Available at: www.aft.org/pdfs/americaneducator/spring2009/WILLINGHAM%282%29.pdf.